CW01373287

This journal belongs to:

_____

_____

_____

_____

The Marriage Course

This journal is designed to be used with The Marriage Course sessions. Please see page 165 for more information on how to join or run a course.

© Alpha International 2020

First edition published 2001

This new edition published 2020
10 9 8 7 6 5 4 3 2

All rights reserved. No part of this guide or any other Alpha publication may be reproduced or transmitted in any form or by any means, electronic or mechanical, including photocopy, recording or any information storage and retrieval system, without permission in writing from the copyright holder or the expressly authorised agent thereof. Where an Alpha publication is offered free of charge the fee is waived on condition the publication is used to run or promote Alpha and should not be subject to any subsequent fee or charge. This resource may not be modified or used for any commercial purpose without permission in writing from the copyright holder or the expressly authorised agent thereof.

ISBN 978-1-7349522-7-8

Unless otherwise indicated, all Scripture quotations taken from the Holy Bible, New International Version Anglicised. Copyright © 1979, 1984, 2011 Biblica, formerly International Bible Society. Used by permission of Hodder & Stoughton Publishers, a Hachette UK company. All rights reserved. 'NIV' is a registered trademark of Biblica. UK trademark number 1448790.

Scripture marked NASB taken from the NEW AMERICAN STANDARD BIBLE®, Copyright © 1960,1 962,1963,1968,1971,1972,1973,1975,1977,1995 by The Lockman Foundation. Used by permission.

Scripture quotations marked NLT are taken from the Holy Bible, New Living Translation, copyright © 1996, 2004, 2015 by Tyndale House Foundation. Used by permission of Tyndale House Publishers, Inc., Carol Stream, Illinois 60188. All rights reserved.

Scripture quotations marked MSG are taken from THE MESSAGE, copyright © 1993, 2002, 2018 by Eugene H. Peterson. Used by permission of NavPress. All rights reserved. Represented by Tyndale House Publishers, Inc.

The teaching on the Five Love Languages is adapted from Dr. Gary Chapman's bestselling book, The 5 Love Languages®: The Secret to Love That Lasts, by Gary Chapman (© 2015). Published by Northfield Publishing. Used by permission. To learn more about Dr. Gary Chapman and to take the free online 5 Love Languages® Profile, visit 5LoveLanguages.com

Published by Alpha International, HTB Brompton Road, London SW7 1JA.
Designed by Birch®, 4 Plantain Place, Crosby Row, London SE1 1YN.

internationalpublishing@alpha.org

Contents

SESSION 1
Strengthening Connection — 06

SESSION 2
The Art of Communication — 24

SESSION 3
Resolving Conflict — 40

SESSION 4
The Power of Forgiveness — 56

SESSION 5
The Impact of Family — 76

SESSION 6
Good Sex — 92

SESSION 7
Love in Action — 110

Follow-on: Tools, Habits and Conversations — 128

Appendices — 145

Acknowledgements — 164

How to use this journal

To help you get the most out of your journal, we have used symbols for specific activities:

When you write something down

When you talk with your partner

When you sit back and reflect

When you note down your intentions – for example, your plans for a date night or hopes for the future

When you swap journals and write something in your partner's journal that will be helpful for them to look back on in the future

Following the course, we hope the journal will serve as a reminder of what you've discovered about each other and the journey you're on as a couple, and help you to put into practice what you have learnt.

Welcome to The Marriage Course...

The course aims to equip you with tools to build a healthy marriage and to strengthen the connection between you as a couple – or to restore that connection if you feel you've lost it.

This journal is designed for you to be able to reflect, to talk and to dream together about your future, not only on the course but afterwards too. There are no right or wrong answers and no one else will see your journals. You won't be asked to discuss anything about your relationship with anybody else. Instead we'll be pausing at various points to allow you as a couple to discuss issues that we've raised.

We want to encourage you, whether you've been together for a short or a long time; whether you're in a good place as a couple or you're struggling – whatever your situation – you've come to the right place. We're confident that, as you engage with the material on The Marriage Course, you'll find out more about what your partner thinks and feels. However long you've been together, there's always going to be more to discover. It's only as we continue on this journey of discovery about each other that we stay connected.

Nicky and Sila Lee
Creators of The Marriage Course

Session 1

Strengthening
Connection

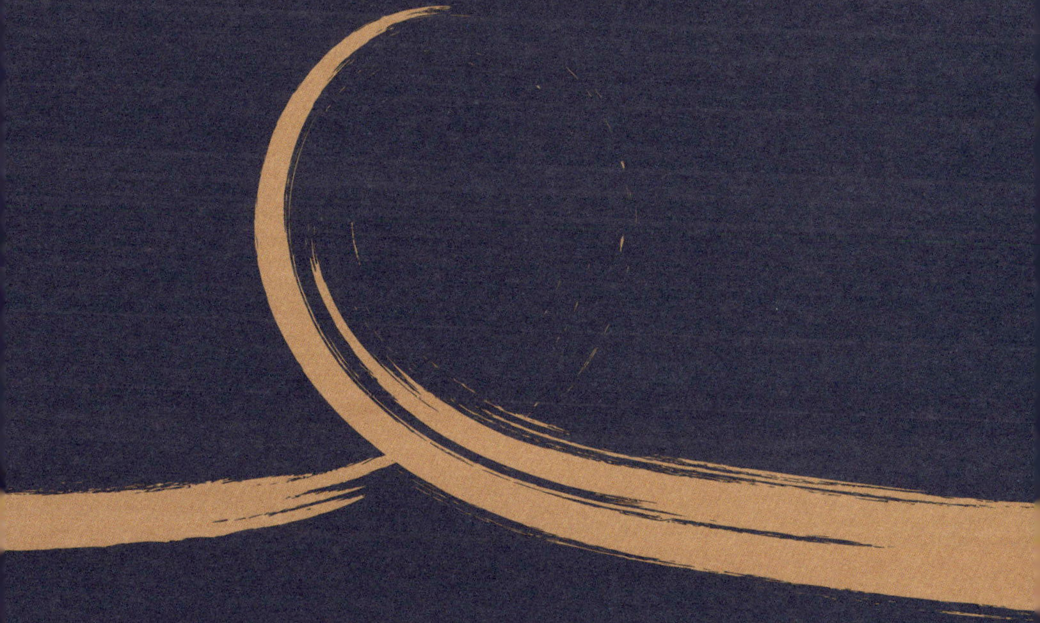

Marriage is designed to be the closest possible relationship of increasing intimacy and growing interdependence. But this is not automatic, we have to keep working at our marriage if we're to stay closely connected.

For this reason a man will leave his father and mother and be united to his wife, and they will become one flesh.
— GENESIS 2:24

Session 1 – Strengthening Connection

CONVERSATION 1
5 minutes

THE FIRST TIME YOU MET
Tell each other your strongest memory of the first time you met and what first attracted you to one another.

Tending a vineyard

Four analogies for tending a marriage:

1. Adjusting

The early years of marriage require a lot of adjustment.

We can change ourselves; we can't change our partner.

2. Pruning

As life gets busier, a key skill in marriage is prioritising our relationship (pruning back certain areas of our lives in order to prioritise another).

There may be pressures on our time from children, work or other demands on us.

We will only survive as a couple if we learn to prioritise our marriage relationship over every other demand on our time.

3. Supporting

Marriages need a support network (eg, friends and family).

We may face challenges from illness, infertility, finances, empty nest, elderly parent(s).

Supporting and encouraging each other is essential.

When we support each other, the very challenges we face can draw us closer together.

4. Renewing

Being prepared to talk about our own individual needs and desires.

Sharing with our partner our hopes for our future together.

Slowing down for long enough to decide on changes we'd like to make.

Possibly stopping certain activities in order to have more time together.

Starting something new that will strengthen or restore or renew the connection between us.

Session 1 – Strengthening Connection

> **If you're struggling in your marriage, we want to encourage you that reconnecting is possible.**
>
> **When couples have tended their relationship, things have changed dramatically and they go on to experience a new connection and intimacy.**

CONVERSATION 2
5 minutes

WORKING THROUGH CHALLENGES
- Talk about any pressures and challenges you've worked through together in the past.
- What are the main pressures either or both of you are facing currently?
- Ask your partner, 'In what ways could I support you in working through this challenge?'

CONVERSATION 3
30 minutes

REVIEWING YOUR CONNECTION

Read through the list of statements and, using the scale below, write in the box the number that you feel corresponds to your viewpoint. Please do it on your own. When you have finished, follow the instructions on the opposite page.

0. never true   1. rarely true   2. occasionally true   3. usually true   4. always true

I feel that...

1. We give each other our undivided attention ☐
2. We understand and support each other's beliefs and values ☐
3. We show each other affection through demonstrative non-sexual touching ☐
4. We are able to apologise and forgive when one of us has hurt the other ☐
5. We listen to each other's point of view even when we disagree ☐
6. We are able to talk about our sexual hopes and desires ☐
7. We are able to talk about our hopes and dreams for the future ☐
8. We are good at encouraging each other in what we each do ☐
9. We make it a priority to go out together at least once a fortnight ☐
10. We reflect on the good things we enjoy as a couple ☐
11. We are able to talk about strong emotions such as excitement, hope, grief and anxiety ☐
12. We are sensitive towards each other's sexual needs ☐
13. We encourage each other's spiritual growth ☐
14. We are good at meeting each other's emotional needs ☐
15. We agree on our sexual practices ☐
16. We discuss new ideas with each other ☐
17. We support each other in the goals we have for our family life ☐
18. We have a number of joint interests that we pursue together ☐
19. We are both happy about the frequency of our lovemaking ☐
20. We are good at listening to each other's feelings without interrupting or criticising ☐

Results of reviewing your connection

1. Add up your scores from the statements on the opposite page as follows:

Statements about:	My score	Partner's score
Your friendship (statements 4, 8, 9, 14, 18)		
Your communication (statements 1, 5, 11, 16, 20)		
Your physical relationship (statements 3, 6, 12, 15, 19)		
Your future together (statements 2, 7, 10, 13, 17)		

2. Now discuss what you have each put, including any differences in your scores (the idea is to be understood by and to understand each other better).

3. Write something for each area that **you** could do to increase your scores:

   Our friendship:
   For example: *'I recognise the need for us to spend time together on our own.'*

   Our communication:
   For example: *'I obviously need to show you that I am interested in what you say.'*

   Our physical relationship:
   For example: *'I would like to be more sensitive towards your sexual desires.'*

   Our future together:
   For example: *'I would like to find a good time for us to have a conversation about our plans for the future.'*

   When you have both finished, show each other what you have put.

Make time for each other

Making time for the people that matter most in our lives doesn't just happen; it requires a conscious decision to make it happen. If a relationship is to thrive and keep growing, we must have regular quality time together.

The benefits of a weekly date:

- keeps the fun and romance alive in our relationship
- deepens our understanding and appreciation of each other
- ensures we communicate regularly on a meaningful level

Plan to spend one to two hours alone together each week to rekindle romance, have fun and talk together about your feelings (your hopes, fears, worries, excitements).

It doesn't need to be expensive.

> **Golden rule:**
> **Never change your date without consulting your partner.**

Session 1 – Strengthening Connection

How to make a weekly date happen:

Plan it into your calendar as you would a business appointment or social engagement

Prioritise it over all other activities (work, friends, sport, TV, children)

Protect it from external demands and pressures on your time, whether people, phones, social media

> By doing so, we're saying to each other, 'You're the most important person to me, and I'm giving you my full attention.'

CONVERSATION 4
5 minutes

SPECIAL TIMES TOGETHER
Tell your partner what have been the most special times you have shared together as a couple. Be specific. Talk about where and when those times were and what you were doing. Explain why they were special to you.

Nurture each other

Nurturing involves seeking to meet each other's emotional needs for affection, encouragement, support, comfort, etc.

It's as though there's an empty space inside that needs to be filled up with another person's love and attention

- when we're known intimately, when we're loved by another, we are no longer alone; the space inside is filled up
- the way to keep filling this space inside is by recognising and meeting each other's emotional needs

> **We are made for close relationships and we all have a longing to be known and to be loved by another person.**

The Lord God said, 'It is not good for the man to be alone.'
— GENESIS 2:18

How to nurture each other

In marriage we can either be reactive or proactive:

- **being reactive is when we focus on each other's shortcomings**

- **being proactive involves focusing on each other's needs**

Proactive behaviour draws us together because each of us feels loved. When we feel loved, we feel like loving.

Study each other and recognise each other's needs. Often our partner's needs and desires will be different to our own.

We can't assume our partner automatically knows our desires. We must tell each other.

> **Discover what matters to your partner. Otherwise, we tend to give what we like to receive.**

Husbands... live with your wives in an understanding way.
— 1 PETER 3:7 (NASB)

CONVERSATION 5
10 minutes

KNOWING ME, KNOWING YOU
Please read through the list on the opposite page.

1. In column A, tick the three that matter most to you (that is, what you would most like your partner to give to you).

2. In column B, tick the three that you believe matter most to your partner (this is, what you think they would most like to receive from you).
   NB: There is some overlap between the different desires – put those three which most clearly express your preferences.

3. When you have both finished, exchange your responses and see how well you understand your partner:

    – How close were you to selecting the three that matter most to your partner?

    – How many of the same desires did you and your partner put for yourselves? 0, 1, 2 or 3?

    – Consider which, if any, of the list of desires you tend to give least to your partner. Are these any of the three that matter most to your partner?

Session 1 – Strengthening Connection

	A Myself (choose 3)	B My partner (choose 3)
Affirmation – being appreciated for who you are by your partner		
Approval – being commended for those things you have done well		
Companionship – doing things together and sharing experiences		
Conversation – talking together about issues of interest and importance		
Encouragement – being inspired to keep going through your partner's words		
Openness – being confident of your partner's honesty about every aspect of their lives, including their feelings and ideas		
Physical affection – the communication of care and closeness through physical touch		
Practical help – experiencing your partner's help in big or small tasks		
Presents – receiving tangible expressions of love and thoughtfulness		
Respect – having your ideas and opinions considered and valued by your partner		
Security – facing the future confident of your partner's commitment to love you and stay with you		
Sexual intimacy – having regular opportunities to express and receive love through your sexual relationship		
Support – knowing your partner is working with you to fulfil your goals		
Time together – knowing your partner has set aside time to be with you on a regular basis		
Understanding – knowing your partner is aware of what matters to you		
Undivided attention – focusing on each other to the exclusion of any distractions		

Continuing the Conversation

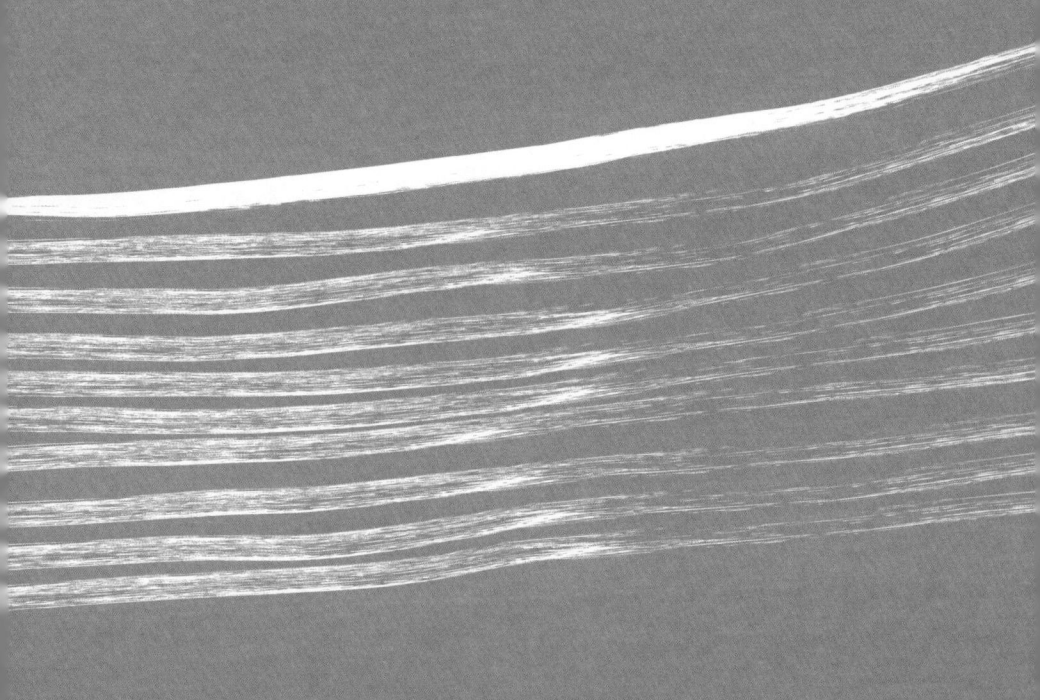

'Prioritising date night is constantly the most difficult thing that we struggle to do, but the most important in terms of how it impacts our relationship.'

— Couple on The Marriage Course

Plan a date together

Be creative: your date doesn't have to look like anybody else's.
Experiment with different times. When could you have a date this week?

	Mon	Tues	Wed	Thurs	Fri	Sat	Sun
Morning							
Afternoon							
Evening							

My turn / your turn to organise what we do.

This week, we could..

The thing that initially attracted me to you was...
(Complete in your partner's journal)

What interests do you have in common?
For example: *visiting art galleries, playing a sport, exploring new places, going to the cinema.*

It may be helpful to think back to some of the things you did when you first got together.

Is there a new interest that you could try doing together?
Think creatively around a new activity, or a sport, or a hobby you could take up together.

What do you enjoy doing separately?
Talk about whether you are allowing each other enough space to pursue these separate interests.

Session 1 — Strengthening Connection

What I love about going on a date with you is...

For example: *time for deeper conversations, having fun, catching up on each other's news, getting to know you better.*

What could potentially prevent us having a weekly date?

Complete the following in your partner's journal

My dream date would be:

Save

Spend

Splurge

Conversation starter on your next date:
Look back to 'Knowing me, Knowing you' on pages 18–19 and ask each other, 'What could I do to meet your top three desires this week?'

Session 2

The Art of Communication

RECAP

On the last session I discovered that my partner's top three emotional needs are for:

1.

2.

3.

(If you can't remember, look back to the Conversation 'Knowing Me, Knowing You' on page 18–19.)

Say to your partner:
'Thank you for meeting my need for.............................. when you...............................'

Find out from your partner what they think is most important for you to stay connected as a couple on a regular basis.

Session 2 – The Art of Communication

We all have a deep longing for emotional connection; it is a fundamental human need.

Emotional connection in marriage will only be achieved where there is good communication.

Effective communication

Different levels of communication
- **Level 1: Passing on information**
- **Level 2: Sharing our ideas and opinions**
- **Level 3: Being open about our feelings and needs**

Level 3 takes vulnerability and requires trust.

Effective communication involves speaking and listening well.

Good communication is multilayered; it involves
- our words
- our tone of voice
- our body language

> **Our aim in marriage should be to listen twice as much as we talk.**

CONVERSATION 1
10 minutes

A SIGNIFICANT MEMORY
– Take it in turns to spend one minute telling your partner about a happy, or some other significant, memory of something that happened to you before you met.

– As you're talking, be sure to express what you felt as you recall this memory. Don't just describe the facts.

– When it is your turn to listen, summarise what you have heard, taking particular care to describe your partner's feelings. This will show you have been listening and empathising with what your partner feels about this memory.

The importance of talking

Important to tell each other our thoughts and feelings

- we may have been taught to hide our feelings during our upbringing

- some people have difficulty recognising what they are feeling (if this describes you, please see the Continuing Conversation 'Identifying Emotions', page 38)

- it takes courage and practice to learn how to talk about feelings

- if your partner finds this hard, help them to feel safe enough to open up

Session 2 – The Art of Communication

CONVERSATION 2
5 minutes

BARRIERS TO TALKING
Take a few minutes to look together at the diagram below and tell each other if any of these barriers apply to you.

- THEY WON'T BE INTERESTED.
- I MAY BE MISUNDERSTOOD
- IT'S NOT IMPORTANT.
- IT MIGHT UPSET THEM.
- I DON'T KNOW WHERE TO START.
- I DON'T WANT TO WORRY THEM.
- I DON'T WANT TO DISTURB THE PEACE.
- I HAVE TO BE STRONG
- IT'S TOO COMPLICATED.
- THEY MIGHT LAUGH AT ME.
- I MAY SOUND WEAK.

Does anything else stop you from opening up and talking?

The importance of listening

Good listening is one of the most important skills to learn for a strong marriage
— listening has great power to make our husband or wife feel loved and valued

> **Research indicates that the average individual only listens for 17 seconds before interrupting.**

CONVERSATION 3
5 minutes

THE POWER OF LISTENING
Discuss the following questions as a couple:

– How do you feel when you are listened to?

– How do you feel when you are not listened to?

– To whom would you go if you needed a listening ear?

– What makes that person a good listener?

> **There is no one who is more important to listen to than our husband or wife.**

Spouting off before listening to the facts is both shameful and foolish.
— PROVERBS 18:13, NLT

Hindrances to listening

Five bad listening habits

1. **Disengaging**
   When we have a separate conversation going on in our head or we're not listening properly because of our physical environment.

2. **Reassuring**
   Not allowing our partner to voice negative emotions.

3. **Giving advice**
   Focusing on solutions rather than empathising with our partner.

4. **Going off on a tangent**
   Taking over the conversation with our own agenda.

5. **Interrupting**
   Failing to let our partner finish what they want to say.

These habits can prevent the speaker from saying what they're feeling, which may eventually cause them to shut down.

We need to listen first before coming in with our contribution.

> **We can all learn the art of effective listening, but it takes time and requires us to be intentional.**

CONVERSATION 4
5 minutes

IDENTIFYING BAD HABITS
Take a few moments to identify your own bad listening habit(s).
Check to see if your partner agrees!

Five steps for reflective listening

1. **Try to put yourself in your partner's shoes**
   Put your own views to one side and really appreciate what it's like for your partner to be feeling the way that they do. Allow your partner to finish what they are saying. Maintain eye contact and do not do something else at the same time. Do not rush them and do not be afraid of silences.

2. **Acknowledge what they've said**
   When you have listened to what your partner wants to say, reflect back what they said without deflection or interpretation. At this stage you're not agreeing or disagreeing or giving your own opinion. (Your turn will come later.)

3. **Find out what is most important**
   Then ask your husband or wife: 'What is the most important part of what you have been saying?' Wait quietly while your partner thinks about what they want to say. When they have spoken, reflect back again what you have heard.

4. **Help them work out what they might do**
   Now ask: 'Is there anything you would like to do (or, if appropriate, like me or us to do) about what you have said?' Again give your partner time to think quietly. When they have finished, reflect back what your partner has said, enabling them to hear their own ideas.

5. **Ask if your partner has said all they need to**
   Don't assume you already know everything your partner wants to say. If there is more, reflect this back too.

> **So often we think being a good conversationalist is all about having interesting views or fascinating stories to tell. But asking the right questions is what enables deep conversation.**

> 'Reflecting back' has two benefits: It helps us find out if we've really understood what our partner has told us and it helps them know if they've been understood... Reflecting back may feel awkward or contrived, but it works!

CONVERSATION 5
30 minutes

REFLECTIVE LISTENING

Each of you pick an issue currently upsetting or bothering you that you have not discussed recently. At this point, choose an issue where there has not already been a lot of disagreement and conflict. It could be an area of concern related to work, holidays, children, your home, etc.

- The speaker should hold a table napkin (or something similar). This is to remind you whose issue is being discussed.
- The speaker tells the listener about the issue and how they feel about it (do not go on for too long). The listener listens and then reflects back.
- Then the listener asks, **'What is the most important aspect of what you are saying?'** The speaker responds. The listener listens and then reflects back again.
- The listener then asks, **'Is there anything you would like to do (or, if appropriate, like me / us to do) about what you have just said?'** Again the listener listens and then reflects back.
- Finally, the listener asks, **'Is there anything more that you would like to say?'** The listener listens and then reflects back again.

Then switch roles so you both have a chance to speak and to listen. This conversation is good practice for all of us, both in talking about our feelings and in listening to each other.

Continuing the Conversation

'If I were to summarise in one sentence the single most important principle I have learned in the field of interpersonal relations, it would be this: seek first to understand, then to be understood.'

— Stephen Covey

Plan a date together

	Mon	Tues	Wed	Thurs	Fri	Sat	Sun
Morning							
Afternoon							
Evening							

My turn / your turn to organise what we do.

This week, we could..

This week you made me feel valued when you...

Conversation starters on your next date:
Ask your partner: When did you last feel... [pick a word]...

encouraged? | discouraged?
understood? | misunderstood?
rejected? | fully accepted?

Write down some other questions as conversation starters:
For example: *What was the best holiday you've ever had?*

When and where do you have your best conversations?

How good is your communication?

1. Areas in our relationship where I feel that we communicate effectively…

2. Things we don't talk about much that I wish we talked about more…

3. Things that we do not talk about at all…

Then, pick an area of your marriage that you haven't discussed in any depth and follow the steps for the Conversation 5, 'Reflective listening' (page 33). Please ensure that both of you are ready to do this.

Take it in turns to be the speaker and the listener.

Don't worry if it feels awkward or contrived at first. Try to follow the steps and recognise how different it feels really listening to your partner and how it feels to be listened to by them.

Some of you may experience a strong emotional reaction to what your partner is saying. Still, try to hear them out and reflect back what they say.

Please turn over

Identifying Emotions

To help those who struggle to identify what they are feeling.

1. **Completing the partial sentences below will help you identify your emotions and become more emotionally aware.**

    Quickly add a few words to describe your feelings (either positive or negative) for each sentence. The lists to the right will help you to get started.

    When we set off on holiday, I feel...
    When we go out with friends, I feel...
    When I'm in a room with people I don't know, I feel...
    When I'm with my parents, I feel...
    When I think of past successes, I feel...
    When I think of mistakes I've made, I feel...
    When I think of the future, I feel...
    When I think of relating to God, I feel...
    When my husband / wife tells me he / she loves me, I feel...
    When my husband / wife and I have a disagreement, I feel...
    When my husband / wife tells me something I've done that's disappointed or hurt him / her, I feel...
    When my husband / wife apologises to me, I feel...

2. **Complete the following sentences**

    I feel most loved when...

    I get angry when...

    I feel happiest when...

    I feel rejected when...

Now show your partner what you have put.

Session 2 — Continuing the Conversation

Positive emotions

accepted	forgiven	relieved
affirmed	free	respected
appreciated	grateful	safe
calm	happy	secure
capable	hopeful	supported
carefree	humbled	sure
comforted	joyful	trusting
confident	loved	understood
content	liberated	valuable
delighted	peaceful	worthwhile
encouraged	positive	
excited	relaxed	

Negative emotions

abandoned	embarrassed	resentful
afraid	exposed	sad
angry	frustrated	scared
anxious	guilty	sorrowful
annoyed	humiliated	unappreciated
apologetic	hurt	unloved
ashamed	insecure	upset
bored	insignificant	used
confused	jealous	useless
cross	lonely	vulnerable
defeated	misunderstood	weak
depressed	nervous	
disappointed	numb	
disgusted	overwhelmed	
disrespected	pressured	
dissatisfied	rejected	

Session 3

Resolving Conflict

RECAP

Complete the following sentences for your partner to read:

'Since having the 'Knowing Me, Knowing You' conversation (page 18–19),

I have appreciated you meeting my need for..

when you..,'

'When you listened to me during the 'Reflective Listening'

conversation (page 33), I felt..,'

Session 3 – Resolving Conflict

Conflict is inevitable in every marriage – all couples disagree. It doesn't mean we have married the wrong person or that the relationship is doomed to failure.

We come into marriage with different backgrounds, desires, priorities and personalities

- it's no good trying to force our partner to do things our way
- with the right tools, addressing the conflict can strengthen the relationship
- in marriage, we are on the same side, the same team

We need to ask ourselves, 'Are there ways I need to change for the sake of our partnership?'

Four principles for handling conflict

1. Remember your partner's positive qualities

Continue to show appreciation for what you love (and admire) about your partner (even while you may disagree passionately about various issues).

The more we concentrate on the things we appreciate about each other, the more appreciative we become of each other.

Make it a daily habit.

> **No marriage can survive a lack of respect, a lack of positive, encouraging words being spoken to each other.**

CONVERSATION 1
10 minutes

SHOWING APPRECIATION

Write down six things you appreciate about your partner. (Be specific: it may be thanking them for what they do, or it may be expressing your appreciation for who they are – try to make it a mixture – looking particularly for things you may have come to take for granted.)

For example: *'I love the way you get on so well with other people.' 'I love the way you're so affectionate towards me.' 'Thank you for working so hard to provide for our family.' 'Thank you for making our home such a welcoming place to be.' 'I really appreciate it that you fill the car up with fuel.'*

1.

2.

3.

4.

5.

6.

When you have both finished, show each other what you have put.

2. Recognise that differences are good

Don't try to change each other.

Learn to accept differences of temperament, personality, upbringing and values.

Maintain a sense of humour.

> **See your marriage as a partnership in which you combine your strengths and support each other's weaknesses.**

Accept one another, then, just as Christ accepted you...
— ROMANS 15:7

CONVERSATION 2
10 minutes

RECOGNISING YOUR DIFFERENCES

Mark against each issue where on the line your partner's and your own preferences each lie, *eg (N = Nicky; S = Sila)*

Money	S		N
	Spend		*Save*
Punctuality	S		N
	Have time in hand		*Cut it fine*

ISSUE	PREFERENCE	
Clothes	Casual	Formal
Disagreements	Thrash it out	Keep the peace
Holidays	Seek adventure	Seek rest
Money	Spend	Save
People	Time with others	Time alone
Phone	Talk at length	Only for making arrangements
Planning	Make plans and stick to them	Be spontaneous/go with the flow
Punctuality	Have time in hand	Cut it fine
Relaxation	Go out	Be at home
Sleeping	Go to bed late	Get up early
Sports	Enthusiast	Uninterested
Tidiness	Keep everything tidy/under control	Be relaxed and live in a mess
TV	Keep it on	Throw it out

Show each other what you have put. Then find one issue where your differences can be a source of strength for your relationship.

Session 3 – Resolving Conflict

3. Look for an 'us' solution

Recognise bad times to discuss disagreements.

The 10 o'clock rule
The 10 o'clock rule can be called into play by either you or your partner if you are having an argument late in the evening. It means the argument has to be paused and postponed until a better time.

Five practical steps:

1. Focus on the issue
   - move the issue from between you and put it in front of you
   - discuss the issue rather than attacking each other

2. Use 'I' statements
   - avoid labelling ('You always...', 'You never...')
   - describe your feelings ('I feel undervalued when...')

3. Listen to each other
   - take it in turns to talk (the speaker holds something, as described in Session 2, to indicate whose turn it is)

4. Brainstorm possible solutions
   - make a list if necessary

5. Decide on the best solution for now and review later
   - if it's not working, try another solution from your list

If you've realised that anger is an issue for you, don't be afraid to seek help. Ask your course leader for information about where to find this.

Why do you look at the speck of sawdust in someone else's eye, and pay no attention to the plank in your own eye?... first take the plank out of your own eye and then you'll see clearly to remove the speck from the other person's eye.
— MATTHEW 7:3,5

CONVERSATION 3
30 minutes

USING THE FIVE STEPS
1. Identify the best times and the worst times to discuss disagreements.

Our best times are...

Our worst times are...

2. Tell your partner which of the five steps you think is the most important for you.

3. Each choose an issue which causes, or could potentially cause, conflict between you.

My issue:

Your issue:

4. Taking one issue at a time, take it in turns to express your point-of-view. The one speaking should hold something, such as a handkerchief, to remind you whose turn it is.

5. Choose one of the issues

Together brainstorm some possible solutions.
(Don't rule out any at this stage. Be aware some may involve one or both of you making a change.)

Choose the best solution for now…

Agree to review the solution in…………weeks.

6. Take the other issue

Together brainstorm some possible solutions.

Choose the best solution for now…

Agree to review the solution in…………weeks.

4. Support your partner

When we expect our partner to meet all our needs, we inevitably fail each other and get hurt, causing our marriage to spiral downwards.

Focus more on meeting your partner's needs rather than expecting them to meet yours.

> **Ask your partner, 'How can I make your day better?'**

When we look to God to meet our needs for unconditional love, we are able to focus more easily on each other's needs (see diagram below).

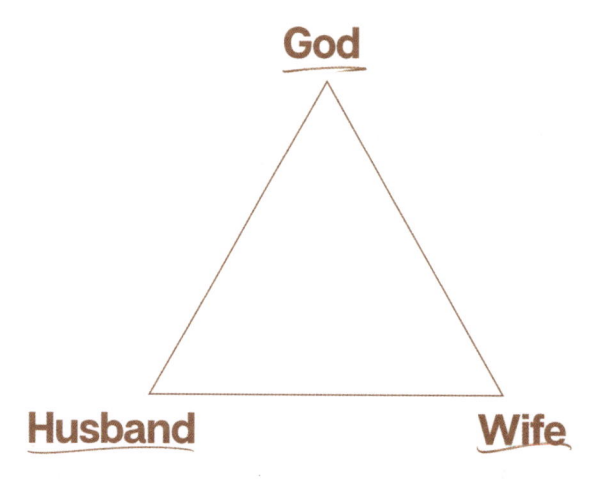

God

Husband   **Wife**

This describes a husband and wife with God at the centre of their relationship. To find out more about the Christian faith, consider doing Alpha together – go to alpha.org to find out more.

God is our refuge and strength, an ever-present help in trouble.
— PSALM 46:1

Session 3 – Resolving Conflict

Praying for each other helps us connect on a regular basis
- five to ten minutes a day is generally better than one hour every month
- ask each other, 'What can I pray for you today?'
- draw on God's promises from the Bible and start with thankfulness
- the closer each of us is individually in our relationship with God, the closer we will be to each other as husband and wife as in the triangle diagram opposite
- if one of you has upset the other, say sorry and forgive each other before praying

> **A cord of three strands is not quickly broken.**
> **ECCLESIASTES 4:12**

If you don't pray, find other ways to support each other on a daily basis

---

CONVERSATION 4
5 minutes

SUPPORTING EACH OTHER
Ask your partner if there's something they're concerned about at the moment. Then, if you're comfortable praying, pray for each other – aloud or silently. Otherwise, express your support in some other way.

What could you do daily to connect and support your partner more?

Continuing the Conversation

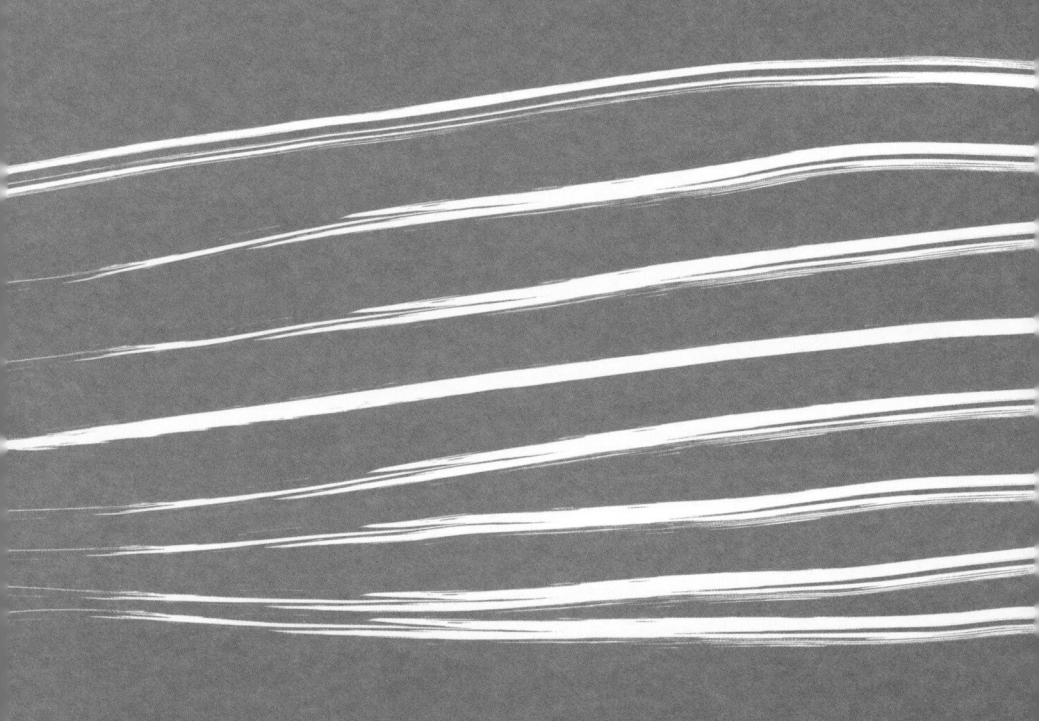

'The problem with some marriages is not that they argue too much, they don't argue enough. They don't let each other know how they feel.'

— Rob Parsons OBE

Plan a date together

	Mon	Tues	Wed	Thurs	Fri	Sat	Sun
Morning							
Afternoon							
Evening							

My turn / your turn to organise what we do.

This week, we could..

What could you do to make your partner feel like he / she is the most important person to you?

Conversation starter on your next date:
Talk about when you have laughed together the most and how you can deliberately create more times of laughing together.

Session 3 — Continuing the Conversation

This week I plan to...
(Write in something kind you could do to make your partner's week better.)

Which of the differences between us is most obviously complementary?

When is a good time / where is a good place to discuss issues that cause us conflict?

The main issue that causes conflict for us is around...

Appendix 1 contains additional conversations to address specific areas of conflict. Go to the relevant page(s) for your area(s) of conflict:

Money and possessions: page 146
Household chores: page 149
How you spend your free time: page 152
Parenting: page 155

Session 4

The Power of Forgiveness

RECAP

The last session showed me that our different approaches to..can be complementary.

Underline or circle whatever's relevant to you from the following list.

I need to remember to:

- organise a date

- meet my partner's emotional need for...

- listen better

- express my feelings more

- focus on the issue causing conflict rather than attacking my partner

- make time to pray together

- tell my partner what I appreciate most about them

Talk about what you have each put.

Session 4 – The Power of Forgiveness

Saying sorry and forgiving each other are vital because we will all hurt our partner.

The hurt must be healed if our marriage is to flourish.

> **Unresolved hurt will undermine the trust and openness between us and destroy our intimacy.**

Reactions to hurt

Anger

Anger is not bad in itself – it has a God-given purpose and is part of our internal mechanism to signal something is wrong and needs to be sorted out.

But we can use anger wrongly in a number of ways.

Two inappropriate ways of managing our anger:

like rhinos	**like hedgehogs**
– they attack when provoked	– they withdraw when threatened

CONVERSATION 1
5 minutes

RHINOS AND HEDGEHOGS
Identify whether you are more like a rhino or more like a hedgehog when you're hurt. If you're not sure, ask your partner.

Unless anger is managed properly, it leads to a downward spiral.

HURT

ANGER

RETALIATION

FEAR

In your anger do not sin. Do not let the sun go down while you are still angry, and do not give the devil a foothold.
— EPHESIANS 4:26

> **An emotion is never buried dead – it is always buried alive.**
> SELWYN HUGHES

What happens if hurt and anger are buried?

Behavioural symptoms
- inability to relax
- low sexual desire
- quick temper / intolerance
- escape through drugs, alcohol, pornography, etc
- escape into work / children / religious activities etc

Physical symptoms
- disturbed sleep
- appetite affected
- medical conditions eg: ulcers, high blood pressure, pain

Emotional symptoms
- loss of positive emotions eg: romance, love, joy
- low self-esteem / depression
- shut down
- fear of confrontation

> Do you notice any of these symptoms in yourself from burying hurt and anger?

CONVERSATION 2
15 minutes

HANDLING ANGER

The purpose of this conversation is to help you recognise how each of you typically responds when you feel hurt and how you display anger.

1. Put a number between 0 and 4 in the box against each statement to indicate how true it is for you. Then add up columns A and B.

   0. never | 1. rarely | 2. sometimes | 3. often | 4. always

When I'm hurt, I...　　　　　　　　　　　　　　　　　　　　A　B

1. Keep the peace at any price
2. Overreact and go on the attack
3. Fail to admit I am angry / hurt
4. Apologise because I must have caused it
5. Become controlling and bossy
6. Give my partner the silent treatment
7. Am quick to blame others
8. Retaliate by becoming confrontational
9. Withdraw or shut down emotionally
10. Want to run away and hide
11. Lose control / become explosive by shouting / slamming doors, etc.
12. Say things I later regret
13. Try to ignore my feelings
14. Become cold and clinical or sarcastic
15. Say things to hurt my partner
16. Withhold physical affection / sex
17. Demand immediate discussion of issue
18. Hurl accusations to take the focus off my responsibility
19. Feel I don't have a right to be angry
20. Bring up past hurt not related to the issue

Total for each column

My score   Partner's score

Column A = Rhino behaviour
Column B = Hedgehog behaviour

Now look at each other's scores and discuss them, especially your differences.

2. At times of disagreement, what words or phrases are you aware that you use, if any, that hurt your partner?

3. What words or phrases does your partner use, if any, that hurt you?
   (This question is especially important if either or both of you recognise that you react like the rhino.)

4. At times of disagreement, are you and your partner able to express your views and feelings?

5. If not, how could you help your partner to do so?
   (This question is especially important if either or both of you recognise that you react like the hedgehog.)

Process for healing hurt

1. Talk about the hurt

Whether you have hurt your partner or have been hurt by them, take the initiative to bring it out into the open so things can be healed.

Small hurts, if left unaddressed, can build up like small stones, which eventually block a drain.

> "
> If… you suddenly remember a grudge [your partner] has against you… leave immediately, go to [your partner] and make things right.
>
> MATTHEW 5:23–24, MSG

> "
> If [your partner] offends you, go and tell them — work it out between the two of you.
>
> MATTHEW 18:15, MSG

2. Say sorry

Take responsibility – resist the urge to make excuses or to blame your partner

> **Making excuses / blaming our partner:** *'I know I criticised you in front of the children yesterday, but I wouldn't have done so if you hadn't made us late.'*
>
> **Proper apology:** *'I hurt you by criticising you in front of the children yesterday; it was unkind of me. I am sorry.'*
>
> **Making excuses / blaming our partner:** *'I know I was grumpy and rude towards you last night, but you don't understand what intense pressure I've been under at work for the last two weeks.'*
>
> **Proper apology:** *'It was selfish and insensitive of me to be rude and grumpy towards you last night. I am sorry to have hurt you.'*

Find out how serious the hurt is for your partner
> – use the 'Richter Scale' of hurt.
> – ask, 'Is this a one or a two level of hurt for you, or is it a nine or a ten?'

Confessing to God and receiving his forgiveness helps us to see the effect of our actions.

> **Apologising opens the way for reconciliation and healing.**

> **A true apology doesn't make excuses.**

CONVERSATION 3
30 minutes

IDENTIFYING UNRESOLVED HURT

This conversation concentrates particularly on identifying the areas of hurt and seeking to understand each other's feelings better. The Continuing Conversation that follows this session focuses on apology and forgiveness.

Part 1 – Try to identify your partner's hurt
Think about ways in which you have hurt your partner and affected your marriage that have not been resolved between you. Think back to when you were going out, when you were engaged and early times in your marriage, as well as recent times. (None of us is perfect.) Ask yourself:
- What have I failed to do that I should be doing?
- What have I done (or am I doing) that I should not do?
- Where have I failed to meet my partner's needs?
- What have I said that has been hurtful?
- What have I left unsaid that could have shown love and encouragement?

Write a list of the things that come to mind. Be specific.
(For example: *'I have stopped being affectionate and rejected your initiatives to make love; I have fallen asleep in front of the television instead of talking with you; I have been out more consistently with work colleagues or friends than we have together as a couple; I said some very unkind things during that big argument we had two weeks ago about money.'*)

Part 2 – Identify your own hurt

Identify the ways in which you have been hurt by your partner. The cause of the hurt could be recent or a long time ago. Your partner might or might not have been aware of hurting you and it could have been one incident or repeated many times. Make sure you are specific and that you describe how you felt.
Use 'I' sentences.

(For example: *'I was hurt when you didn't say anything special about my promotion; I haven't got over the fact that you lied to me on the night we first went out together; I feel frustrated because you don't discuss financial decisions with me.'*)

1. When you have both finished, exchange your lists.
2. Read silently the ways you have hurt each other.
3. One of you then 'reflect back' to your partner the reason for their hurt and the feelings it produced in them, without trying to interpret what they have written or to defend yourself. To clarify what they feel, ask questions such as, *'What did you mean by that?'* Or, *'Is there anything else you would like to say?'*
4. Then the other partner should 'reflect back' in the same way. Make sure each of you has an understanding of the feelings that are described.
5. Return the lists to each other. Then add to or revise your list of the ways you have hurt your partner. Spend some time considering every aspect of their hurt. Try to see it through your partner's eyes.
6. Through the coming week, ask God to give you new insights into why your partner feels hurt and your part in causing it.
7. It is important to complete the process of *'getting rid of bitterness, rage and anger'* (Ephesians 4:31) by apologising and forgiving if you haven't already done so. (Use the Continuing Conversation, 'Healing Unresolved Hurt' on pages 73–75 to do this if necessary.)

3. Forgive

Forgiveness is essential and one of the greatest forces for healing in a marriage.

Forgiveness is, first and foremost, a choice, not a feeling:
- forgiveness always costs us something
- the question is not, *'Do we feel like forgiving?'* but, *'Will we forgive? Will we let go of our self-pity / demand for justice / desire to retaliate?'*

Forgiveness IS NOT:
- pretending that the hurt doesn't matter and trying to forget about it
- denying the hurt (and just hoping it will go away)
- thinking, *'Our love for each other will somehow magically resolve any ways we hurt each other, so it doesn't matter'*

Forgiveness IS:
- facing the wrong done to us
- recognising the emotions inside
- choosing not to hold it against our partner

Forgiveness is a process – we often need to keep forgiving for the same hurt, sometimes on a daily basis.

> **Forgiveness goes beyond human fairness: it is pardoning those things that can't readily be pardoned at all.**
> – C.S. LEWIS

Get rid of all bitterness, rage and anger... Be kind and compassionate to one another, forgiving each other, just as in Christ God forgave you.
— EPHESIANS 4:31–32

Session 4 – The Power of Forgiveness

Think of a time when you have been forgiven or when you have forgiven someone. How did it make you feel?

What do you find hardest about forgiving?

Start again together

Begin each day with a fresh start.

Don't expect healing to be instant – apology and forgiveness remove the distance between us but the hurt leaves a bruising that needs time to heal.

Rebuild trust by setting aside some quality time together and being gentle and kind towards each other.

CONVERSATION 4
5 minutes

COMFORTING EACH OTHER
Ask your partner what you can do to help them with this process of healing. Then, if you feel comfortable, pray for each other – aloud or silently. Otherwise express comfort for your partner in some other way.

> **Love keeps no record of wrongs.**
> — 1 CORINTHIANS 13:5

Confess your faults to one another and pray for one another that you may be healed.
— JAMES 5:16

Continuing the Conversation

'Where there is forgiveness at the heart of a marriage, it has unparalleled power to bring healing.'

— Nicky and Sila Lee

Plan a date together

	Mon	Tues	Wed	Thurs	Fri	Sat	Sun
Morning							
Afternoon							
Evening							

My turn / your turn to organise what we do.

This week, we could..

This week I really appreciated it when you...

What is the most helpful response from your partner when you tell them that you are feeling hurt?

Do you find it easier to say sorry or to forgive? Why is that?

Session 4 — Continuing the Conversation

Healing unresolved hurt

It is important to complete the process of healing any hurt between you that you identified in Session 4 on pages 66 and 67, if you haven't already done so. (Keep using the conversation below whenever you identify hurt between you in the future.)

My partner's deepest hurt happened when I..
(look at what you wrote on page 66)

My partner felt ridiculed / humiliated / unaffirmed / put down / criticised / rejected / unloved / undervalued / ....

From now on, I intend to..

I intend not to..

If appropriate, write a prayer expressing to God your regret, asking for his forgiveness and praying for his help not to repeat the behaviour that hurt your partner.

For example: *Lord, thank you that you help those who call out to you. I am so sorry for hurting my partner by..........................I ask you to forgive me and to help me to change so that I do not cause them further hurt. Please heal our relationship and show me how to express love to my partner.*

Please turn over

Say sorry to your partner
'I am so sorry for...
I know it hurts you and makes you feel...
From now on I intend to...
Please forgive me.'

When you feel ready, express forgiveness to your partner for what they have expressed.
Say, 'I forgive you for ....'

If you are finding this hard, ask God for his help. It may help to write down your prayer.

For example: *Dear Lord, thank you that you know all about me and love me. Thank you for being ready to forgive me for the ways I have hurt others. You know how hurt and angry I felt when my partner criticised me when I'd done my best. I choose to let go of my anger and resentment. I want to put my desire to retaliate into your hands, and ask you to help my partner to change. I choose to forgive him / her as you have forgiven me. Please heal the hurt with your love.*

Comfort each other

This is important when you have made yourselves vulnerable to each other and helps to bring healing to the hurt.

If you're comfortable praying, pray that your partner will know freedom from guilt and shame.

Then think of something you both enjoy that you could do together for a date this week to replace the negative emotions with positive ones.

Conversation starter on your next date:

Do you think that your wider family is made up of more rhinos or more hedgehogs?

How did this play out / does this play out in your wider family relationships?

Session 5

The Impact of Family

RECAP

Tell your partner:

'You're really good at' (choose one)

- prioritising our date night
- meeting my need for... (see 'Knowing Me, Knowing You' on pages 18–19)
- talking about how you feel
- listening to me without interrupting, criticising or offering advice
- saying what you appreciate about me
- discussing the issue rather than attacking me when we disagree
- supporting me by...
- not holding on to hurt and anger
- apologising
- forgiving me

Then say to them:

'I need to work on' (choose one)

- prioritising our date night
- meeting your need for... (see 'Knowing Me, Knowing You' on pages 18–19)
- talking about how I feel
- listening to you without interrupting, criticising or offering advice
- saying what I appreciate about you
- discussing the issue rather than attacking you when we disagree
- supporting you by...
- not holding on to hurt and anger
- apologising
- forgiving you

Session 5 – The Impact of Family

> How would you describe your family background?

Family background has a big influence on a marriage
- for some people, the support they receive from their family is good and helpful in building a strong marriage
- for others, it's more complicated and can even be damaging

Leaving and letting go

When we get married, a profound change should take place in our relationship with our parent or parents (or whoever were our main caregivers as we grew up)
- the change from being a child and completely dependent upon them to a healthy independence as an adult
- the significance of leaving is not so much the physical move as the psychological and emotional one
- we create **a new 'centre of gravity'** – our highest loyalty must be to each other

Support each other.

If necessary, put boundaries in place, not to cut yourselves off from your parents but to connect with them as a couple in a new way.

> **Listen to parental advice but make your own decisions together as a couple.**

For this reason a man [and a woman] will leave their father and mother and be united to [each other]...
— GENESIS 2:24

CONVERSATION 1
10 minutes

CURRENT RELATIONSHIPS

– Talk about your current relationships with wider family members.

– Discuss in what ways these relationships are a source of strength and support in your marriage.

– Then see if you can identify anything that's causing tension and what changes you could make.

Building healthy family relationships

1. Resolve any conflict

Use the same process as in Session 4 to unblock the drain:

- identify and talk about the main issue causing tension
- apologise when you have been wrong
- choose to forgive and move on

2. Consider their needs

Focusing on what irritates us pushes us apart.

Focusing on another person's needs draws us together.

It can be helpful to take the initiative with parents about things like:

- visiting them
- enabling them to see their grandchildren
- working out what holidays you might spend together
- phoning them

Honour your father and your mother...
— EXODUS 20:12

Session 5 – The Impact of Family

CONVERSATION 2

10 minutes

SUPPORTING YOUR PARENTS

1. How could you express your gratitude towards your parents (and / or your parents-in-law)?

2. How can you best keep in touch with your parents (and / or parents-in-law)? Consider telephone calls, timing and length of visits, and other ways of communicating with them.

3. Consider the needs of your parents and parents-in-law, or other family members. From the list below, tick the relevant boxes for their needs. Beside the boxes you have ticked, write the ways you could help meet those needs.

Husband's parent(s) (or other family members)	Needs	Wife's parent(s) (or other family members)
☐	Advice	☐
☐	Companionship	☐
☐	Conversation	☐
☐	Encouragement	☐
☐	Practical help	☐
☐	Security	☐
☐	Understanding	☐
☐	Other Need	☐
☐	Other Need	☐

Looking at our past

We bring a mixture of experiences into our marriage from our family background:

- what was good (be grateful for that)
- what was different to our partner's experience (be aware that this can cause conflict)
- what was negative (and may be painful)

A healthy home involves providing a **secure base** from which children can explore, and a **safe haven** to which they return to have their emotional needs met.

> **Buried hurt and anger from our past can come out against our partner.**

Is there anything negative from your upbringing that is influencing your relationship with your partner?

If it is possible, as far as it depends on you, live at peace with everyone.
— ROMANS 12:18

Session 5 – The Impact of Family

CONVERSATION 3
30 minutes

REFLECTING ON YOUR UPBRINGING
A. Your immediate family relationships
The big circle drawn below represents yourself. Draw circles to represent the relationship between members of your immediate family as you were growing up.

- If there was some relationship (some communication but not close), make the circles touch
- If there was a close relationship (good, open communication and conflict well resolved), overlap the circles
- If there was a lack of relationship (divorced, separated or no communication), separate the circles

Then look at each other's arrangement.

For example:

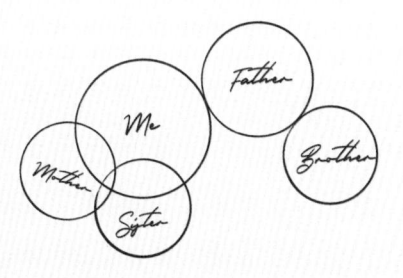

Please turn over

B. Your parents' / step-parents' (or main caregivers') relationship with you

Please consider the following questions and tick the relevant boxes:

Did your parents or step-parents...	Mother/Step-mother (tick if Yes)	Father/Step-father (tick if Yes)
praise you as a child?	☐	☐
meet your physical needs (for food, clothes, home, etc)?	☐	☐
give you a sense of security?	☐	☐
respect your uniqueness?	☐	☐
encourage you in your development?	☐	☐
set clear rules / appropriate boundaries for you?	☐	☐
give you increasing freedom appropriate to your age?	☐	☐
comfort you when you were upset?	☐	☐
give you presents?	☐	☐
take an interest in your life?	☐	☐
treat their children equally?	☐	☐
admit their mistakes and apologise when necessary?	☐	☐
forgive you for your mistakes?	☐	☐
have realistic expectations of what was appropriate for your age?	☐	☐
accept your friends?	☐	☐
help you relate well to your siblings and peers?	☐	☐
establish clear family rules?	☐	☐
give discipline in a consistent, fair way?	☐	☐
spend ample time with you (ie, play with you, talk to you, etc)?	☐	☐
show you physical affection (ie, hug you, kiss you, etc)?	☐	☐
give you a sense of a 'secure base' to go out from?	☐	☐
provide a 'safe haven' for you to return to?	☐	☐

C. Your parents' / step-parents' (or main caregivers') relationship with each other

Did your parents or step-parents...	Yes	Sometimes	No	Don't Know
have a strong loving relationship?	☐	☐	☐	☐
show interest in each other?	☐	☐	☐	☐
have fun together regularly?	☐	☐	☐	☐
spend time together on their own?	☐	☐	☐	☐
show each other physical affection?	☐	☐	☐	☐
help each other in small or big tasks?	☐	☐	☐	☐
encourage each other with praise and appreciation?	☐	☐	☐	☐
show each other respect?	☐	☐	☐	☐
communicate honestly and directly?	☐	☐	☐	☐
listen to each other without interrupting or criticising?	☐	☐	☐	☐
resolve conflicts effectively?	☐	☐	☐	☐
apologise to and forgive each other when appropriate?	☐	☐	☐	☐
agree on the use of their money?	☐	☐	☐	☐
give each other presents?	☐	☐	☐	☐
have mutual interests?	☐	☐	☐	☐
show a willingness to negotiate?	☐	☐	☐	☐
remain faithful to each other?	☐	☐	☐	☐

Please turn over

When you've finished A, B and C above, please discuss the following questions together:

- Can you identify aspects to be grateful for from your upbringing?
- Did you have any unmet childhood needs?
- Are you aware of these adversely affecting your marriage?
- Are you aware of benefits to your marriage / family life through imitating your parents / step-parents / main caregivers?
- Are you aware of ways you adversely affect your marriage / family life through imitating your parents / step-parents / main caregivers?

Healing childhood pain

1. Grieve your own and your partner's unmet needs

You may encounter strong feelings as you do this, but recognising and admitting to yourself the hurt you've experienced can be a huge step forward.

Allow your partner to talk about what has been lost and give them the gift of your emotional support.

2. Forgive

Give up continuing expectations and longings of what you have wanted your parents or others to be for you.

Remember, forgiveness is an ongoing act of the will and is essential for healing.

> **Forgiving someone is not condoning their actions or giving them the right to repeat what they've done. Forgiveness is about being set free from the ways they've hurt you.**

Rejoice with those who rejoice; mourn with those who mourn.
— ROMANS 12:15

Forgiveness can be expressed as part of a prayer:
- nothing is beyond God's power to heal and restore
- pray for yourself and each other
- ask God to heal the sense of loss and to help you to know his love
- dwell on the promises of God in the Bible
- believe God's unconditional love for you as you are now
- do not use childhood pain as an excuse for not meeting your partner's needs

CONVERSATION 4
5 minutes

COMFORTING EACH OTHER
- If this is a hard area for your partner, ask them, 'What's the most painful part for you?'

- Reflect back what they tell you to show you're with them in this.

- Then ask your partner for one way you could support them. If you're comfortable praying, pray for each other. Otherwise, express your support in some other way.

I have loved you with an everlasting love and am constant in my affection for you.
— JEREMIAH 31:3

Continuing
the Conversation

'Addressing issues about our background together means we will understand better where each other is coming from and then work together to create our own unique marriage culture.'

— Nicky and Sila Lee

Plan a date together

	Mon	Tues	Wed	Thurs	Fri	Sat	Sun
Morning							
Afternoon							
Evening							

My turn / your turn to organise what we do.

This week, we could..

This week you made me smile when...

What were the positive aspects of the family you grew up in?

What were the negative aspects of the family you grew up in?

What are the big differences between your upbringings?

Session 5 — Continuing the Conversation

I am grateful to you for the ways our marriage has brought healing to childhood loss and pain...

Think about one way you can support your parents, your in-laws or another family member this week.
– For a further conversation about building healthy relationships with your wider families, turn to Appendix 3, page 161.

Conversation starter on your next date:
Tell each other your vision for the kind of relationship and family life you hope to have moving forward?

(This may be very different to the home either of you grew up in.)

Session 6

Good Sex

RECAP

Ask your partner what was most important for them from the impact of family on the last session?

One thing we could each do to improve our relationships with our families is...

Session 6 – Good Sex

> **Emotional connection creates good sex, and good sex creates a greater emotional connection.**

Sex is the ultimate body language through which we communicate our desire for our partner; for:

- closeness
- comfort
- love
- protection
- wanting to have a child together

Our sexual relationship:

- restores our emotional wellbeing, which helps us cope with the pressures of life
- expresses and deepens the 'one flesh' bond
- is dependent on the emotional connection between us

What does sex mean to you?

I am my lover's and my lover is mine...
— SONG OF SONGS 6:3

Five secrets for keeping the spark alive
S.P.A.R.K.

1. Speaking

Difficult at first because it is deeply private and requires vulnerability.

Tell each other what you enjoy – don't leave it to guesswork.

Most couples struggle with their sexual relationship at one time or another

- 40% of women and 30% of men will experience a sexual problem at some point

> **Don't regard any issues in your sexual relationship as 'your' issue or 'my' issue but 'our' issue.**

CONVERSATION 1
10 minutes

UNDERSTANDING EACH OTHER

– Discuss with your partner whether you grew up with positive or negative messages about sex.

– Tell each other whether your upbringing made it easy or difficult for you to talk about your sexual relationship now.

2. Prioritising

Guard the physical space for your lovemaking:

- leave screens outside the bedroom
- invest in an alarm clock if necessary

Be creative:

- vary the atmosphere – soft lighting can help
- vary how you make love
- vary who takes the initiative
- approach variety with sensitivity at a mutually agreeable pace
- our attitude should be to seek to give pleasure to our partner and not just take it for ourselves

> **Sex isn't just the icing on the cake of a marriage – it's an important ingredient of the cake itself.**

What creative change could you make in the bedroom to improve your sex life?

3. Anticipating

Our most potent and important sexual asset is our mind.

Having your own private language and private signals around sex spark thoughts that create anticipation and build desire (the best sex starts at breakfast!).

Mutually agreed periods of sexual abstinence can enhance a couple's sexual relationship.

Romance creates the setting for lovemaking.

Be sure sexual thoughts and desires are directed towards your partner.

> **Romance is the bridge between the everyday world of practicality and the private place of our sexual relationship.**

Visit **themarriagecourse.org** to see recommended books for building a good sexual relationship and for help on issues relating to pornography addiction.

Finally, brothers and sisters, whatever is true, whatever is noble, whatever is right, whatever is pure, whatever is lovely, whatever is admirable – if anything is excellent or praiseworthy – think about such things.
— PHILIPPIANS 4:8

CONVERSATION 2
10 minutes

MOST ROMANTIC MOMENTS
– Tell each other what have been the most romantic moments for you in your relationship, whether that's recently or when you first met.

– Listen carefully as it will help you create romance in the future.

4. Responding

Sex often starts as a decision and then arousal follows.

Responding sexually can give our partner a sense of confidence and wellbeing.

Giving ourselves sexually requires a climate of trust.

> What stops you from responding positively when your partner initiates sex?

'...at our door is every delicacy, both new and old, that I have stored up for you, my lover.'
— SONG OF SONGS 7:13

5. Kindness

Sex is about giving

   – showing support in practical ways and taking time to tune in to each other's emotional needs

Men and women are wired differently when it comes to sexual arousal.

Be 'OTHER-oriented' rather than SELF-oriented'.

Our kind words will build confidence in our partner

   - never criticise your spouse's natural shape

   - keep telling each other what you love about their body

What is one way you could show kindness to your partner for the sake of your sexual relationship?

There is a very strong link between building each other's self-esteem and building an intimate sexual relationship.

His left arm is under my head, and his right arm embraces me.
— SONG OF SONGS 2:6

CONVERSATION 3
30 minutes

TALKING ABOUT SEX
A. Rate your lovemaking
Circle a number for each of the five qualities – first for yourself (A) and then for your partner (B) – which you feel best describes your sexual relationship, where 1 = not so good and 5 = very good:

A. You	Qualities	B. Your partner
1 2 3 4 5	Speaking	1 2 3 4 5
1 2 3 4 5	Prioritising	1 2 3 4 5
1 2 3 4 5	Anticipating	1 2 3 4 5
1 2 3 4 5	Responding	1 2 3 4 5
1 2 3 4 5	Kindness	1 2 3 4 5

Which area(s) do you need to work on?

B. Identify any problem areas
1. What, if any, are the differences between you, as husband and wife, in the way you respond sexually?

   Are these differences having a positive or negative effect on your marriage?

   If positive, give the main reason:

   If negative, give the main reason:

Please turn over

2. Does your self-esteem and body image affect your lovemaking negatively?
   If so, explain why:

   How could your partner help you?

3. What, if any, unresolved emotions (for example: *resentment, hurt, unforgiveness, anxiety* or *guilt*) affect your lovemaking in any way?

   How could these be resolved?

4. Does your lovemaking lack excitement?
   If so, what new element would you like to see introduced?

5. Does over-tiredness take a toll on the frequency of your lovemaking?
   If so, identify the reason for over-tiredness:

   What could re-energise you? (For example: *conversation, better communication, resolving past hurt, planning and prioritising sex, more sleep, less going out, more fun and less work*)

6. Do you feel free to talk together about your lovemaking?
   If so, write down two or three things your partner has told you recently that have enhanced your lovemaking:

   If the answer is no, identify some of the reasons for your difficulty:

   Suggest something you would like your partner to say that you have never heard:

7. What are the main romance killers for you?

C. Write the script

List below the different criteria that would create good lovemaking for you.

Be specific about things such as timing, taking the initiative, anticipation, position, atmosphere, place, romance, tenderness, seduction and arousal (foreplay), afterwards. (We cannot guess each other's expectations.)

1.
2.
3.
4.
5.
6.
7.
8.
9.
10.

D. Seek to understand each other better

- Once you have finished, read each other's responses to Sections A, B and C.
- Now start to talk about what the other has expressed – beginning where you feel most comfortable.
- Give each other the opportunity to ask questions about what you have written. Tell your partner what surprised you most. Ask for clarification if you do not fully understand.

Protecting our marriage

Practical steps to affair-proof our marriage:

1. Build each other up
The most common cause of affairs is a failure to meet each other's emotional needs.

> **It's our emotional connection with each other that ultimately maintains our sexual attraction to each other.**

2. Set boundaries
Infidelity starts and stops in the mind.

We can't help being attracted to other people, but we can decide whether or not to entertain such thoughts.

Many affairs begin not with immediate sexual attraction but through intimate conversation.

3. Talk to someone
If feelings become overwhelming, tell your partner or someone else. This can help burst the bubble.

4. Keep sex alive
Normal to have different levels of desire at times.

Loving involves giving to each other – sometimes making an effort, sometimes showing restraint.

As we increase emotional intimacy, physical desire usually increases.

Sometimes we need go back to the basics of enjoying touching and being touched.

So guard yourself in your spirit and do not break faith.
— MALACHI 2:15

CONVERSATION 4

5 minutes

SUPPORTING EACH OTHER

- Tell your partner what was important for you in this session.

- Say sorry to each other for any ways you've spoilt your sexual intimacy and, if appropriate, express forgiveness.

- Ask your partner how you can support them this week. If you feel comfortable, pray for each other, aloud or silently. Otherwise express your support in another way.

Place me like a seal over your heart, like a seal on your arm; for love is as strong as death, its jealousy unyielding as the grave. It burns like blazing fire, like a mighty flame. Many waters cannot quench love; rivers cannot wash it away. If one were to give all the wealth of one's house for love it would be utterly scorned.
— SONG OF SONGS 8:6–7

Continuing
the Conversation

'You have to continually discover and rediscover new ways to keep your sexual energy alive... It doesn't just happen. You have to make it happen. You have to decide to make having a vibrant, exciting, emotionally satisfying sexual relationship a priority.'

— Michele Weiner Davis, TEDx speaker on The Sex-Starved Marriage

Plan a date together

	Mon	Tue	Wed	Thurs	Fri	Sat	Sun
Morning							
Afternoon							
Evening							

My turn / your turn to organise what we do.

This week, we could..

This week you made me feel so loved when you...

One thing I will change to improve our sex life...

Emma Waring's three top tips to help you prepare for making love

1. One of the biggest barriers to sex is tiredness. Rather than expending a lot of energy shopping and cooking, why not agree to get a takeaway one evening or order something in? This will create a sense of occasion and give you more time to prepare.

2. Consider sending flirtatious text messages to your partner, such as, 'Guess what underwear I have on.' Even if your partner is busy and can't respond in kind, they can send a short flirtatious message back, which creates fun and builds anticipation.

3. Both take a shower or bath as soon as you get home from work. This will help you to wash away the cares of the day. Then get into some comfortable clothes or nightwear to set the tone.

Plan times of making love (even if it seems contrived at first) to fulfil what you both feel comfortable with from Section C of the conversation 'Talking About Sex' (page 103). Happiness and fulfilment in this area of our marriage will depend on meeting our partner's needs, as we would like them to meet ours. Be careful not to push your partner to fulfil your desires – look to meet theirs.

Conversation starter on your next date:
The most romantic thing you have ever done for me is...

Session 7

Love in Action

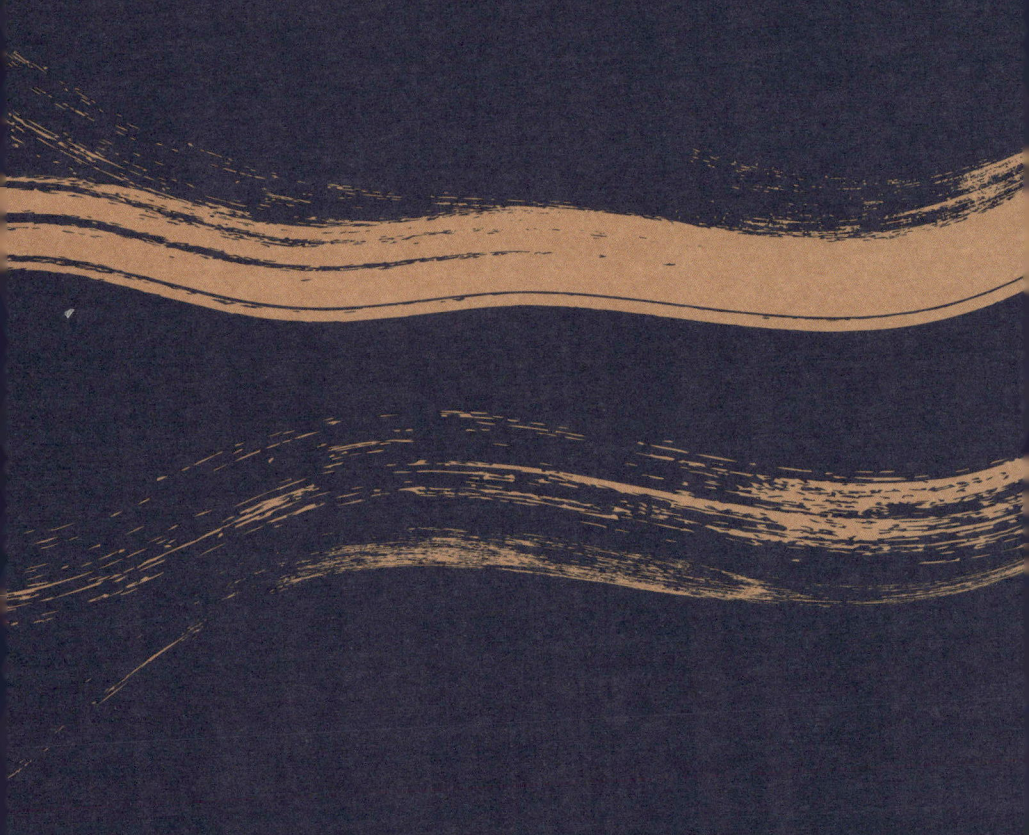

RECAP

Ask your partner:

'What do you think has been the most important thing for our relationship from the course so far?'

Then tell them:

'Last week I realised the best thing I can do to improve our sex life is...'

Session 7 – Love in Action

> Love is about more than feelings; it's about what we do – it involves action. Love always costs us something.

The five love languages[1]

1. Loving words

2. Thoughtful presents

3. Physical affection

4. Quality time

5. Kind actions

For each of us, one of these 'love languages' will communicate love more effectively than the others.

Most people have different love languages to their partner.

> Often we try to communicate love in the way we understand it and want to receive it.

A marriage that is full of love is where we are seeking to meet our husband or wife's needs in the particular way that makes them feel loved.

Using our partner's love language may feel unnatural and awkward initially.

---

[1] The teaching on the Five Love Languages is adapted from Dr Gary Chapman's bestselling book, *The 5 Love Languages®: The Secret to Love That Lasts* (© 2015). Published by Northfield Publishing. Used by permission.

1. Loving words

Words have great power either to build up or to put down our partner.

Give compliments and encourage each other daily.

Speak kindly to each other.

For some people, hearing words of affirmation feels like arriving at an oasis in a desert.

> **"**
>
> **Words affect love. And without loving words, relationships begin to die.**
>
> ROB PARSONS, OBE

Pleasant words are a honeycomb, sweet to the soul and healing to the bones.
— PROVERBS 16:24

2. Thoughtful presents

> **Presents are visual symbols of love.**

Giving presents is a way of investing in our marriage

- can be inexpensive but have high value; for example: a single flower, a bar of chocolate

- don't wait only for special occasions

- actively discover what your partner likes (within your budget!)

CONVERSATION 1
10 minutes

FAVOURITE PRESENTS
Tell your partner what have been the best presents you've received from them. Explain why.

3. Physical affection

Affectionate touch is a powerful communicator of love in marriage

- if this is your partner's primary way of feeling loved, in times of crisis touch will communicate more than anything else that you care

We need to use the whole range and find out from our partner what's appropriate at different moments: holding hands, putting an arm round each other's shoulder or waist, a kiss, a hug, a hand on a hand, a back massage, sexual foreplay, making love

- both sexual and non-sexual touch are important in marriage

> **To touch my body is to touch me. To withdraw from my body is to distance yourself from me emotionally.**
>
> DR GARY CHAPMAN

4. Quality time

Married couples can spend a lot of time together without using it to convey love to each other.

Togetherness means more than physical proximity

- it involves focusing our attention on our partner

Session 7 – Love in Action

Quality time together builds friendship through:

1. Talking together
Important to share our thoughts, feelings, hopes, fears, disappointments.

I need to   ☐ **talk more**   ☐ **listen more**

2. Eating together
Make the effort to initiate conversation.

Ask questions that the other will enjoy answering.

Our meal times would be improved if I...

3. Having fun together
Friendship is built around shared experiences and shared memories.

CONVERSATION 2
10 minutes

TIMES TOGETHER
Each write a list of what you have most enjoyed doing together in the past or perhaps would like to start doing together:

Show each other what you have put. Use your lists as ideas when planning your future dates.

5. Kind actions

This involves expressing love through serving our partner, through seeking to meet their needs in practical ways.

Find out from your partner what kind actions are most meaningful for them.

> **When you're both busy, ask your partner, 'Is there something I can do to help you?' It doesn't always have to be fair.**

Do to others as you would have them do to you.
— LUKE 6:31

Session 7 – Love in Action

Learning to love

Jesus Christ showed love in all five ways:

1. Words
   'As the Father has loved me, so have I loved you.'
   John 15:9

2. Time
   'Come with me by yourselves to a quiet place.'
   Mark 6:31

3. Actions
   'He poured some water into a basin and began to wash his disciples' feet.'
   John 13:5

4. Touch
   'Jesus reached out his hand and touched the man.'
   Luke 5:13

5. Presents
   'Jesus took the loaves, gave thanks, and distributed to those who were seated as much as they wanted.'
   John 6:11

> **Love is not just a feeling – it requires an act of the will to meet each other's needs. We are called to imitate the love of Jesus.**

My command is this: love each other as I have loved you.
— JOHN 15:12

CONVERSATION 3
30 minutes

DISCOVERING YOUR LOVE LANGUAGES

Please do questions 1 and 2 on your own and share your responses before filling in questions 4 and 5.

1. Write down up to 12 specific occasions through which you have known your partner's love for you. (It could be at any stage in your relationship – before or after marriage. These may be regular or rare events and could be deemed of major or minor significance.)

   I have known your love for me when...
   For example:
   'We sat under the stars talking about our future when we were going out.'
   'You gave me that watch on our wedding anniversary.'
   'You cooked a special meal for my birthday.'
   'You said how proud you were of me when I was promoted.'
   'You spontaneously put your arm around me when we were waiting for the film to start.'

   1.
   2.
   3.
   4.
   5.
   6.
   7.
   8.
   9.
   10.
   11.
   12.

2. Taking into consideration your answers to question 1, put the five ways of showing love in order of importance for you, where 1 = most important and 5 = least important. Then consider in which order of importance you think they come for your partner.

For you (number 1–5)	Love languages	For your partner (number 1–5)
	Loving words Thoughtful presents Physical affection Quality time Kind actions	

3. Now, compare and discuss with your partner what each of you put for questions 1 and 2.

4. Looking at your partner's number one 'love language' (ie, the most important for them), list three ways in which you could communicate love to your partner this week or this month. (Try to keep within the bounds of reality!)

    1.

    2.

    3.

5. Looking at your partner's second 'love language' (ie, the second most important for them), list three more ways in which you could communicate love to your partner effectively this week or this month.

    1.

    2.

    3.

Go online to **www.5lovelanguages.com** to fill in a short questionnaire to confirm the order of importance of these love languages for you.

The adventure of love for a lifetime

Marriage is a journey; it's designed to be a dynamic relationship that keeps changing and developing.

Expressing our commitment to each other is essential to the success of the journey.

Commitment is liberating as it means we can:

- take a long view
- plan our future together
- look beyond current difficulties

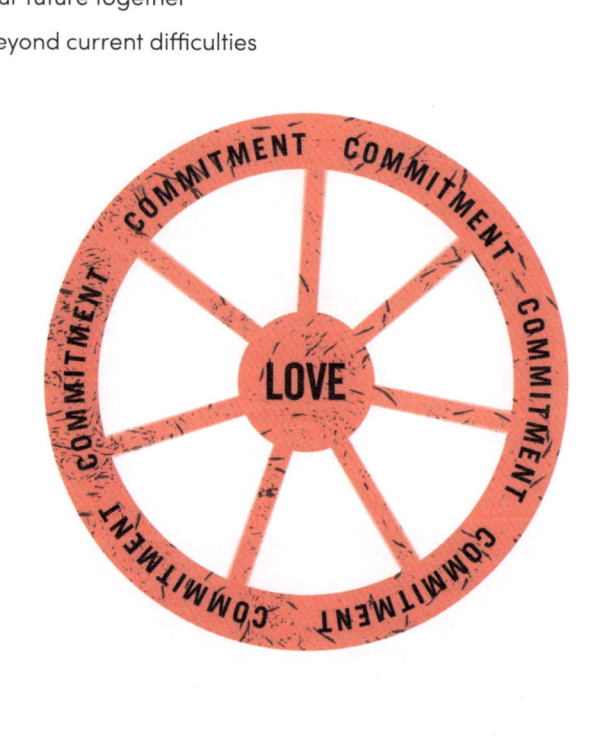

Love does not consist of gazing at each other, but in looking together in the same direction.
— ANTOINE DE ST EXUPÉRY

Session 7 – Love in Action

> **"**
>
> **Every marriage is a really big commitment to the people. It's a commitment that says, 'I'm prepared not only to spend the rest of my life with you, but to spend the rest of my life finding out about you. There's always more of you to discover.'**
>
> DR ROWAN WILLIAMS (FORMER ARCHBISHOP OF CANTERBURY)

CONVERSATION 4

5 minutes

SUPPORTING EACH OTHER

– Ask your partner if there's something particular regarding your future together for which they'd like your understanding and support.

– If you feel comfortable, say a prayer for each other, aloud or silently. Otherwise, express your support in some other way.

Love and faithfulness meet together...
— PSALM 85:10

Continuing the Conversation

'A marriage that is full of love is where we are seeking to meet our husband or wife's needs in the particular way that makes them feel loved.'

— Nicky and Sila Lee

Plan a date together

	Mon	Tues	Wed	Thurs	Fri	Sat	Sun
Morning							
Afternoon							
Evening							

My turn / your turn to organise what we do.

This week, we could..

Ideas for our dates this month...

1.
2.
3.
4.

Write in your partner's journal a kind action that you would really appreciate this week.

Putting the course into practice

Five things I especially want to remember and practise from The Marriage Course:

1.
2.
3.
4.
5.

Show each other what you have written.

Five things you would like me to remember and practise from The Marriage Course? Write them below:

1.
2.
3.
4.
5.

Conversation starter on your next date:
Now we have finished the course, how can we maintain a date night routine?

What is the best sort of date to help us connect as a couple?

How can we make it happen?
For example: *putting boundaries around work, finding a babysitter, budgeting etc.*

Tools, Habits and Conversations

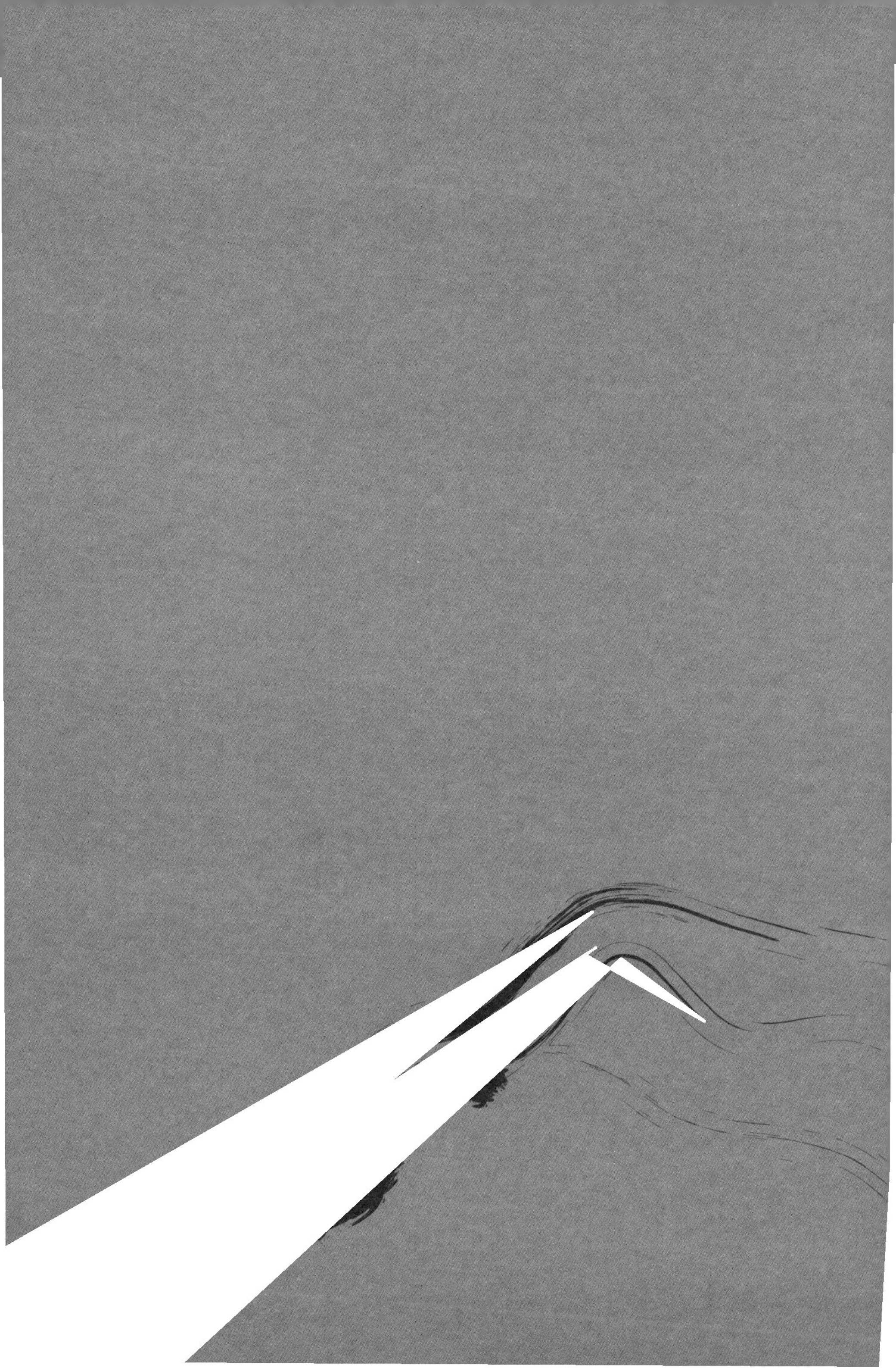

Week 1: Good times together

Plan a date together

	Mon	Tue	Wed	Thur	Fri	Sat	Sun
Morning							
Afternoon							
Evening							

My turn / your turn to organise what we do.

This week, we could..

GOLDEN RULE: Never change your date without consulting your partner.

> **Date night for us is a fun time, when we're relaxing and doing something different to our normal routine. Sometimes it's during the day, but usually it's in the evening for at least two hours around a meal.**
>
> NICKY AND SILA LEE

and Conversations

When I first saw you on our wedding day I felt...

Conversation starter on your next date:
Ask each other, 'What have been the best dates we've been on together?' Why were those times together so enjoyable for you?

Week 2: Communicating well

Plan a date together

	Mon	Tue	Wed	Thurs	Fri	Sat	Sun
Morning							
Afternoon							
Evening							

My turn / your turn to organise what we do.

This week, we could..

> Two people can be living in the same house, sleeping in the same bed, yet, if they don't communicate at the level of their feelings, they can be like strangers towards each other.

Week 2 – Tools, Habits and Conversations

I love talking about...

I find it difficult to talk about...

Have a conversation using the 'Reflective Listening' tools (page 33). Take it in turns to choose an issue you haven't discussed recently.

Conversation starter on your next date:
Ask each other, 'If money and time was no object, what would be your ideal holiday destination?' Get specific! What kind of place would it be? Where would you eat? What would you do all day?

Week 3: Handling disagreements

Plan a date together

	Mon	Tues	Wed	Thurs	Fri	Sat	Sun
Morning							
Afternoon							
Evening							

My turn / your turn to organise what we do.

This week, we could..

Three things I love about you...

1.
2.
3.

Week 3 – Tools, Habits and Conversations

One key difference between us is…

Discuss how this can be a strength, not a weakness, in your relationship.

One area I could make an effort to change for the sake of our relationship is…

Conversation starter on your next date:
Ask each other, 'What good traditions or habits have we created in our marriage?' If you can't think of any, talk about how you could create some traditions that are unique to you. They may seem relatively trivial but they will build special memories in your marriage.
For example: *an early morning swim each New Year's Day; a takeaway every Wednesday; going away on a particular weekend every year; creating a playlist for each other's birthdays.*

Week 4: Keeping the drain clear

Plan a date together

	Mon	Tues	Wed	Thurs	Fri	Sat	Sun
Morning							
Afternoon							
Evening							

My turn / your turn to organise what we do.

This week, we could..

This week I appreciated it when you...

When you feel hurt, are you able to tell your partner?

Do you think it is important to actually say the words 'I'm sorry' (without making excuses) and 'I forgive you'?

This process of forgiveness will eventually become second nature but, until you get used to it, it can be helpful to follow the steps in the forgiveness session:

1. Talk about the hurt
2. Say sorry
3. Forgive

If one of you is feeling hurt by your partner, work through the 'Healing Unresolved Hurt' conversation on page 73.

Conversation starter on your next date:
Tell your partner what you see in them that you don't see in anyone else. Tell them things that you are grateful to them for, things you admire in them and things that you see as emerging qualities in them.

Week 5: Wider family relationships

Plan a date together

	Mon	Tue	Wed	Thur	Fri	Sat	Sun
Morning							
Afternoon							
Evening							

My turn / your turn to organise what we do.

This week, we could..

> **When we support one another and put in a right boundary, it gives us a great sense of emotional closeness and it prevents family members from driving a wedge between us.**

You make me feel so valued when you...

Week 5 – Tools, Habits and Conversations

What did you discover on the course about the differences between your families?

What changes have you agreed to put in place to better support / improve your relationships with your parents / in-laws / wider family?

Conversation starter on your next date:
Ask each other, 'What does your ideal weekend look like?' If it seems your weekends are more geared to one of you than the other, talk about how you could balance it out and do more of the things that the other one likes to do.

Week 6: Strengthening your physical connection

Plan a date together

	Mon	Tues	Wed	Thurs	Fri	Sat	Sun
Morning							
Afternoon							
Evening							

My turn / your turn to organise what we do.

This week, we could..

I feel so loved when you...

Week 6 - Tools, Habits and Conversations

Based on your Continuing Conversation on page 108, talk about what you each can do to make your sexual relationship more enjoyable for your partner.

I feel in the mood for sex when you...

> **Tell each other what you enjoy - don't leave it to guesswork.**

Conversation starter on your next date:
What has been the season in our relationship when we've had the most fun together? Why do you think that was? What was happening at that time? How could we engender more fun and more laughter in our relationship now?

Week 7: Using the love languages

Plan a date together

	Mon	Tue	Wed	Thur	Fri	Sat	Sun
Morning							
Afternoon							
Evening							

My turn / your turn to organise what we do.

This week, we could..

> Love is about what we do - it involves action and is a choice we make for the sake of another person that will always cost us something.

Go back to Conversation 3 on page 120

My main love languages are...

Your main love languages are...

Week 7 – Tools, Habits and Conversations

Ask your partner to complete the sentence for you:
One thing I could do to make you feel loved is...

Ask each other:
When have your different love languages caused misunderstanding between you?

To ensure my partner feels loved in the future, I will regularly...

Conversation starter on your next date:
What do you think will help us most to keep having regular dates in 10, 20 or 30 years' time? What difference will it make in our marriage?

Appendix 1

Resolving common areas of conflict

The following four exercises help couples recognise the reasons behind common areas of conflict:

Money and possessions: page 146
Household chores: page 149
How you spend your free time: page 152
Parenting: page 155

Complete and discuss together the exercise(s) relevant to you.

Exercise 1 – Money and possessions

1. **Each of you circle the phrases that best describe your feelings (and the messages you received from your family) about money and possessions as you grew up.**

Scrimped and saved Had everything we wanted Had everything we needed	Broken things mended Broken things thrown away	Always short of money Always enough money
Worried about family running out of money No worries about money	Encouraged to give money / possessions away Saved as much as possible	Enjoyed shopping – seen as a leisure activity Shopping kept to a minimum
Money spent only on essentials Money spent on luxuries	Credit cards made use of Credit cards avoided	Loved getting presents Loved giving presents
Took plenty of time to relax Adults always working	Taught how to save money Not taught how to save money	Confident handling money Confusion or fear about money
Felt self-sufficient as a family Money / bills caused arguments	Family finances remained a mystery Family finances explained	As a child given allowance / taught to handle money Adults handled all money

Appendix 1 – Resolving common areas of conflict

Other significant words / phrases that describe your attitude to money and possessions now:

Show each other what you have put and discuss any differences.

2. **Our values regarding money and possessions (ie what is most important to us).**

   For example:
   1. Not worrying about money
   2. Honesty
   3. Generosity
   4. Saving as much as possible
   5. Sticking to our budget

Write your own list before looking at your partner's and writing your 'agreed list'.

My list	Our agreed list
1.	1.
2.	2.
3.	3.
4.	4.
5.	5.

Please turn over

Exercise 1 (continued)

3. **Write down an area of conflict regarding money and possessions. Together write down any possible solutions you can think of. Then put your agreed solution for now.**

For example:

Issue	Possible solutions	Agreed solution for now
Car keeps breaking down	Buy another car now Spend enough money to mend the car properly Change the car in 6 months Use public transport Find a different mechanic Change the car the next time it breaks down	Find a different mechanic

Issue	Possible solutions	Agreed solution for now

Exercise 2 – Household chores

1. **Each of you circle the phrases that best describe your feelings (and the messages you received from your family as you grew up) about household chores.**

Housework shared – no traditional gender roles Traditional roles (eg mother cooked; father did maintenance) Employed a cleaner / other household staff	Grew up in city (with no garden) Grew up in suburbs (some outdoor work) Grew up in country / on a farm (lots of outdoor work)
Chores assigned in an organised manner Children not expected to help around the house Children responsible for many household chores	Parent(s) did a lot of DIY projects / maintenance Parents preferred to call contractor when things needed repair
Grew up in neat, organised home Grew up in messy, disorganised home	Confident with DIY projects Uncomfortable with DIY
House cleaned and tidied regularly Allowed mess to accumulate and then cleaned	Take turns to do chores as and when needed (relaxed approach) Prefer to divide chores and have fixed roles Create a chart for who does what
Enjoyed helping around the house as a child Disliked helping around the house as a child	Enjoy cooking Do not enjoy cooking *Please turn over*

Exercise 2 (continued)

Other significant words / phrases that describe your attitude to household chores:

Show each other what you have put and discuss any differences.

2. Our values regarding household chores (ie what is most important for us).

For example:
1. Share household chores equally
2. Make our home feel 'lived in' and relaxed
3. Pay for household maintenance
4. Keep our home clean and tidy
5. Limit the amount of time we spend on household chores and DIY

Write your own list before looking at your partner's and writing your 'agreed list'.

My list	Our agreed list
1.	1.
2.	2.
3.	3.
4.	4.
5.	5.

Appendix 1 – Resolving common areas of conflict

3. Write down an area of conflict regarding household chores. Each write down any possible solutions you can think of. Then put your agreed solution for now.

For example:

Issue	Possible solutions	Agreed solution for now
Both husband and wife are employed full-time – who does the cleaning?	Do chores as needed – whoever has the time Create a chart, assigning chores to each person Take turns each week / weekend Employ someone to clean the house Do chores together at weekends Assign some chores to older children	Create a chart to assign chores and employ a cleaner to come in once each week
Issue	Possible solutions	Agreed solution for now

Exercise 3 – How you spend free time

1. Each of you circle the words or phrases that best describe your feelings (and the messages you received from your family as you grew up) about how to spend free time.

Structured and planned Flexible and spontaneous	Preferred spending summer holidays staying with wider family Preferred holidays spent at home	Weekends well planned Weekends relaxed and casual Weekends used for socialising Weekends used to catch up on chores
Relaxing, low activity holidays High activity holidays Play a lot of sport on holiday	Luxury travel Budget travel	TV watched infrequently TV a central part of family life
Enjoyed having guests in our home Preferred not having many guests in our home	Involved in many sports / activities Hobbies / intellectual pursuits important Not involved in many activities or sports	Mealtimes central to family life No importance attached to mealtimes
Parents went out together frequently without children Parents stayed at home and we had fun together as a family	Public holidays spent at home Public holidays spent visiting family	Most free time spent as a couple Most free time spent as an individual Most free time spent with friends and family
Ate most meals at home Ate many meals in restaurants	Spent a lot of time with extended family Rarely saw extended family	Morning person – get up early and go to bed early Evening person – sleep in late and stay up late

Appendix 1 – Resolving common areas of conflict

Other significant words / phrases that describe your attitude regarding how you like to spend your free time:

Show each other what you have put and discuss any differences.

2. **Our values regarding free time (ie what is most important to us).**

   For example:
   1. Structured / planned
   2. Travelling together
   3. Mealtimes important
   4. Entertain friends in our home
   5. Time to pursue individual hobbies

Write your own list before looking at your partner's and writing your 'agreed list'.

My list	Our agreed list
1.	1.
2.	2.
3.	3.
4.	4.
5.	5.

Please turn over

Exercise 3 (continued)

3. **Write down an area of conflict regarding how you spend free time. Each write down any possible solutions you can think of. Then put your agreed solution for now.**

For example:

Issue	Possible solutions	Agreed solution for now
Where to spend Christmas	Visit family further away Divide holiday between family time and time on own Host both families at home Go away for Christmas Choose destination / resort for families to meet together Take turns each year visiting different sides of the family	Spend Christmas alone at home and then travel to see extended family after Christmas Day

Issue	Possible solutions	Agreed solution for now

Appendix 1 – Resolving common areas of conflict

Exercise 4 – Parenting

1. **Each of you circle the words or phrases that best describe your feelings (and the messages you received from your family as you grew up) about parenting.**

Strict / disciplinarian Relaxed / informal Balance of love and firm boundaries	Lots of affection and expressions of love Little affection and expressions of love	Encouraging / accepting Performance-based and somewhat critical
No arguing in front of children A lot of arguing in front of children	Encouraged to express negative emotions Stoic and non- emotional	Spanking used to discipline 'Time out', grounding and other forms of discipline used Children allowed to do what they liked
Attended church and prayed together Did not regularly attend church or pray together	Parents very involved in children's activities Parents not very involved in children's activities	Encouraged as children to be increasingly independent Sheltered – independence not encouraged
Money invested in education No money available to invest in education No desire to invest in education	Pressure to achieve Relaxed and allowed to find own level	Calm and quiet – disagreements avoided Disagreements aired with much discussion and passion
Allowed as much screen time as liked Limited on amount of screen time allowed	Regularly spent time as a family having fun together Rarely had fun together as a family Dreaded being together as a family	

Please turn over

Exercise 4 (continued)

Other significant words / phrases that describe your attitude to parenting:

Show each other what you have put and discuss any differences.

2 Our values regarding parenting (ie what is most important for us).

    For example:
    1. Set clear boundaries for the children
    2. Be affectionate (lots of hugs and kisses)
    3. Spend regular time together as a family having fun
    4. Support each other in front of the children
    5. Pass on spiritual values

Write your own list before looking at your partner's and writing your 'agreed list'.

My list	Our agreed list
1.	1.
2.	2.
3.	3.
4.	4.
5.	5.

Appendix 1 – Resolving common areas of conflict

3. **Write down an area of conflict regarding parenting. Each write down any possible solutions you can think of. Then put your agreed solution for now.**

For example:

Issue	Possible solutions	Agreed solution for now
How to balance work and raising children – should both parents work outside home?	*One parent works part-time* *One parent works from home* *Mother stays at home with children until they go to school* *Father stays at home with children*	*Mother stays at home with children until they go to school and then returns to work*

Issue	Possible solutions	Agreed solution for now

Appendix 2

Creating a budget

(see also *The Marriage Book*, Appendix 3: 'Working out a budget')

Money management tips from CAP:

Create a budget

Agree a budget together and stick to it. It might sound simple, but this is the easiest way to keep track of how much money you have and exactly what you're spending it on.

Save, save, save!

Even if you can only afford to save a small amount each month, eventually it all adds up. Having a savings pot you can dip into when facing unexpected costs could be a lifesaver. What about planning ahead for specific things like Christmas?

Do your research

If you've been with the same supplier for over a year, the chances are you're paying more than you need to for energy. By researching the different options available, you can find the cheapest deal that suits your individual needs.

Pay with cash

Pay with cash instead of card. By handing over physical money, you can stay aware of what you're buying. This also means that when the money's gone, it's gone, which might make you think twice about that thing you 'really need'.

If you want to find out more about Christians Against Poverty, visit us at capuk.org.
To book on to a CAP Money Course in your area visit **capmoneycourse.org**.

Appendix 2 – Creating a budget

Monthly Budget Planner

Average monthly income (work out annual figure)
Joint salaries — £..................
Other sources of income — £..................
Total (1) £.......................... ÷ 12 — £..................
(monthly)

Fixed regular expenditure (work out annual figure)	**Actual**	**Budget**
Rent/mortgage	£..................	£..................
Council tax	£..................	£..................
Services (gas, electricity, water)	£..................	£..................
Insurance	£..................	£..................
Loan repayment	£..................	£..................
Travel (season ticket)	£..................	£..................
Car – tax, insurance	£..................	£..................
Charitable giving	£..................	£..................
Other	£..................	£..................
Total (2) £.......................... ÷ 12	£.................. (monthly)	£.................. (monthly)

Flexible 'essential' expenditure (estimate annual figure)		
Household (food, chemist etc)	£..................	£..................
Clothes / shoes	£..................	£..................
Car running costs	£..................	£..................
Telephone	£..................	£..................
Other	£..................	£..................
Total (3) £.......................... ÷ 12	£.................. (monthly)	£.................. (monthly)

Flexible 'non-essential' expenditure (estimate annual figure)		
Entertainment / hospitality	£..................	£..................
Presents	£..................	£..................
Sport / leisure	£..................	£..................
Holidays	£..................	£..................
Going out	£..................	£..................
Other	£..................	£..................
Total (4) £.......................... ÷ 12	£.................. (monthly)	£.................. (monthly)

Monthly sum for savings/emergencies
Total (5) — £.................. £..................

**Add together total monthly expenditure
(2, 3, 4, 5)** — £.................. £..................

Compare to total monthly income (1) — £.................. £..................

Appendix 3

Building healthy relationships with our wider families

A. Being aware of our past

Spend 10 minutes filling in your 'Life Graph' overleaf (example below).

- record the most significant events that come to mind

- put positive experiences above the 'neutral line', between 0 and +100

- put negative experiences below the 'neutral line', between 0 and −100

- show your partner what you have put

- tell your partner what you felt then and what you feel now about these events

- where one of you has been hurt by others during your upbringing, check that you are both going through the steps for 'Healing childhood pain' (page 86)

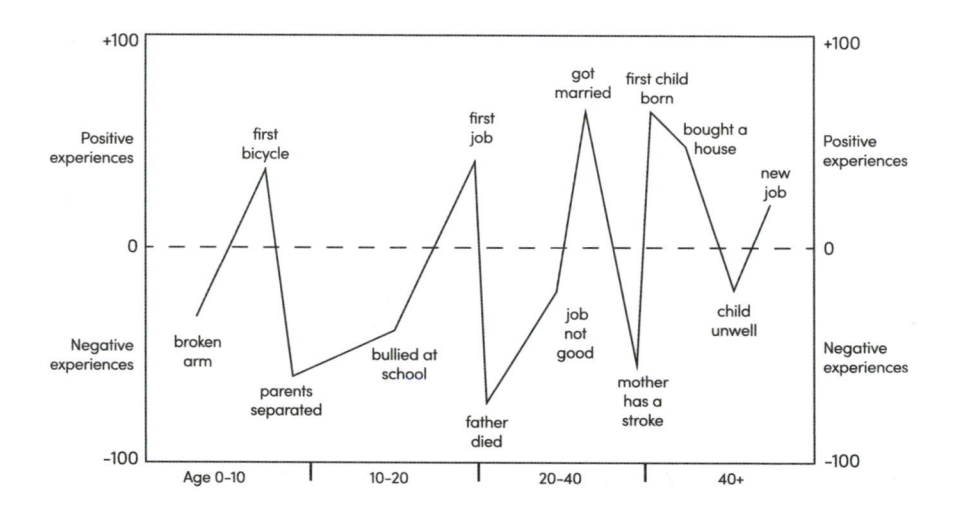

Appendix 3 – Building healthy relationships with our wider families

B. Maintaining healthy boundaries

Each of you should fill in the following questions on your own, and then exchange your answers. Please consider carefully what your partner has written. Discuss the significant issues – pay particular attention to an issue that your partner has highlighted and you have not. You may need to adjust some of your own answers as a result.

1. Do your parents (seek to) control or interfere in your decisions and the direction of your lives? If so, specify the ways.

2. Have you ever noticed an unhealthy emotional dependence between you and a parent, or your partner and a parent? If so, in what way?

3. Are there issues relating to your parents (in-law) that cause tension or arguments between you?
   For example: *'There is often tension between us when I have spent a long time on the phone with one of my parents.'*

4. In what way could you support your partner with regard to your parents and in-laws?

5. In what way could your partner support you with regard to your parents and in-laws?

6. Do you or your partner have unmet childhood needs?
   a) If so, how could you help your partner?

   b) How could your partner help you?

Life Graph

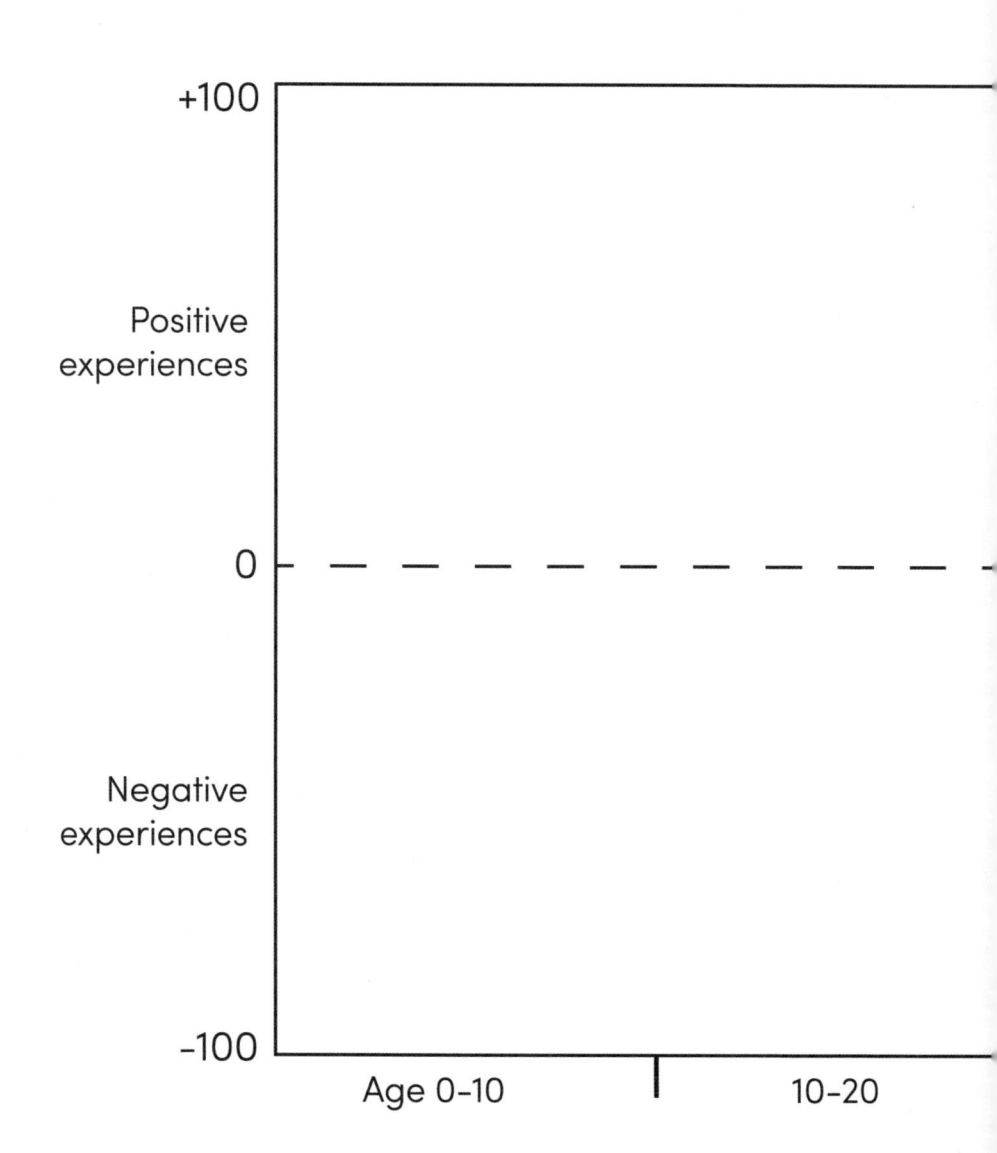

+100

Positive
experiences

0 — — — — — — — —

Negative
experiences

−100

Age 0–10   10–20

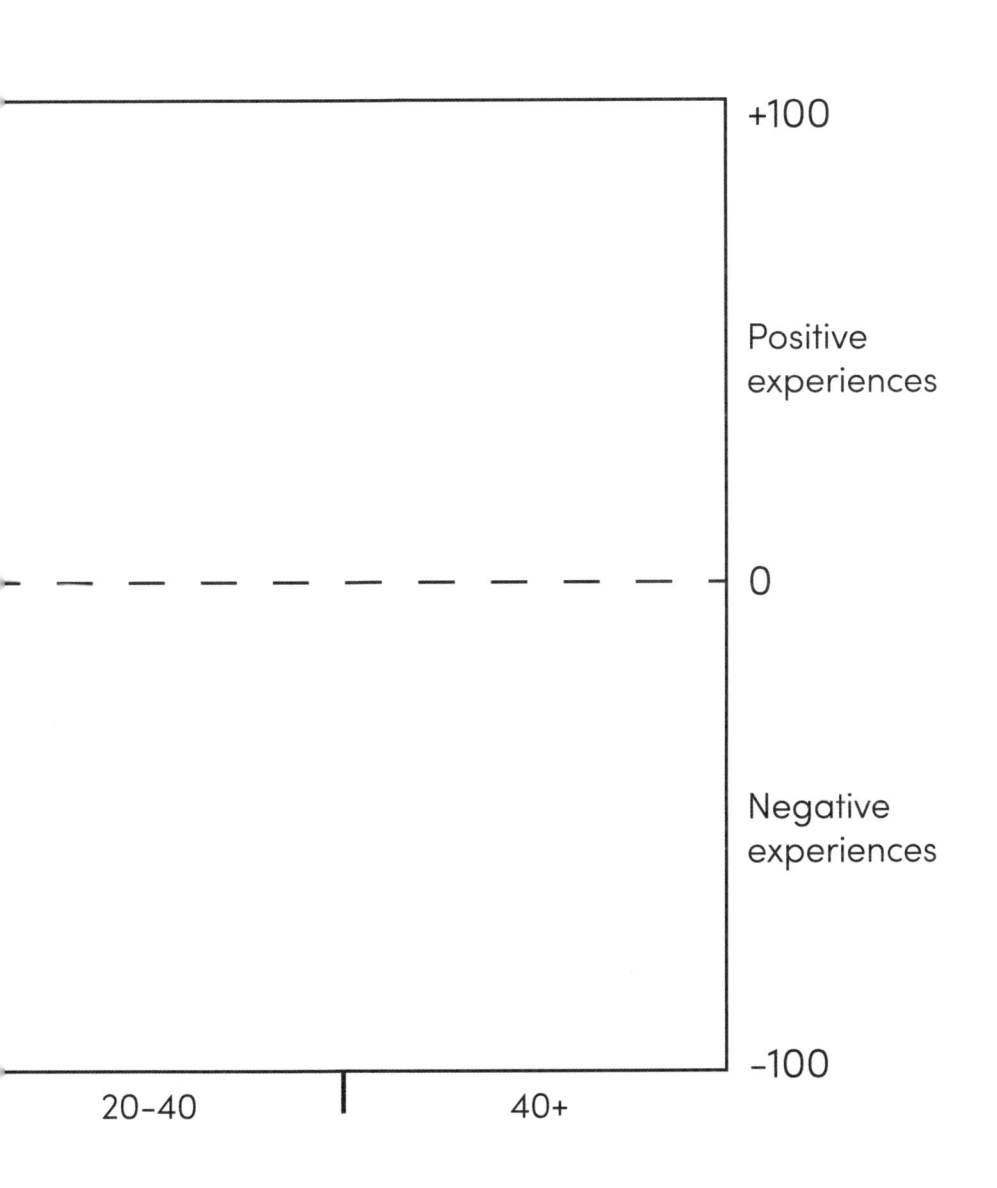

Appendix 3 – Building healthy relationships with our wider families

	+100
	Positive experiences
	0
	Negative experiences
	-100

20-40   40+

Acknowledgements

We are very grateful indeed to the following people and organisations for their valuable contributions to The Marriage Course:

Dr Roger Bretherton, Psychologist, University of Lincoln

Dr Gary Chapman, author of *The Five Love Languages®*, for his book on which the concept and journal notes for Session 7 are based.

Dr Henry Cloud, Psychologist and co-author of *Boundaries in Marriage*

Dr Mosun Dorgu, Child and adolescent psychiatrist

Dr Sue Johnson, Clinical Psychologist and author of *Hold Me Tight*

John Kirkby CBE, Founder of CAP (Christians Against Poverty). For more infomation about this organisation visit capuk.org

Rob Parsons OBE, Founder of Care for the Family, for his inspiration, stories and illustrations that we have used throughout. For more information about his work, please visit careforthefamily.org.uk

Dr Xuefu Wang, Psychotherapist and founder of the Zhi Mian Institute for Psychotherapy

Emma Waring RGN, Psychosexual Therapist and Author

David and Teresa Ferguson, of Intimate Life Ministries, whose expertise and encouragement have helped us enormously, especially with Sessions 1 and 4. For more information about their work, contact: Intimate Life Ministries, 2511 S. Lakeline Blvd, Austin, Texas, TX78759; or visit greatcommandment.net

Peter and Barbie Reynolds, for their demonstration of effective listening, the inspiration for the model example in Session 2.

Acorn Christian Foundation, for their Just Listen! course, on which much of the material on listening in Session 2 is based. For more information about their work, please visit acornchristian.org

For further resources and support or if you are interested in running this course visit **www.themarriagecourse.org** or email info@themarriagecourse.org

If you are interested in finding out more about the Christian faith and would like to be put in touch with your nearest Alpha, visit **www.alpha.org**

Notes

Notes

Notes

Notes